PLANT-BASED ALCHEMY

MESO
· · · · · · · · · · · · · · ·
AMERICAN
· · · · · · · · · · · · · · ·
HEIRLOOM OF
· · · · · · · · · · · · · · ·
NUTS & SEEDS

LATIN AMERICAN FUSION COMPANION

THIS BOOK
IS YOUR COMPANION

The *CollectorCollect team* wants to thank you for welcoming this recipe book into your collection. We're thrilled that this book will become a treasure in your hands. We hope it will inspire your kitchen adventures and bring joy to your gatherings.

This Culinary Collector's Journal transcends mere pages and tips; it invites your creative spirit to venture beyond the familiar and daringly blend new flavors. Embark on a creative quest to explore the profound legacy of Mesoamerican gastronomy today.

We envision this journey book as a steadfast companion in your creative exploration, unlocking endless culinary possibilities. Imagine your kitchen as a sanctuary where you'll craft unique concoctions, each dish and drink a testament to your flair. Let this guide be the canvas for your ideas and memories, transforming every meal and beverage into cherished moments.

Gather your loved ones at the table. Here, connections deepen, stories unfold, and joy is abundant. Together, let's celebrate the art of shared meals, where every dish is more than food—a bridge between cultures, a dance of flavors, and a tribute to the ancient wisdom that informs our modern culinary endeavors.

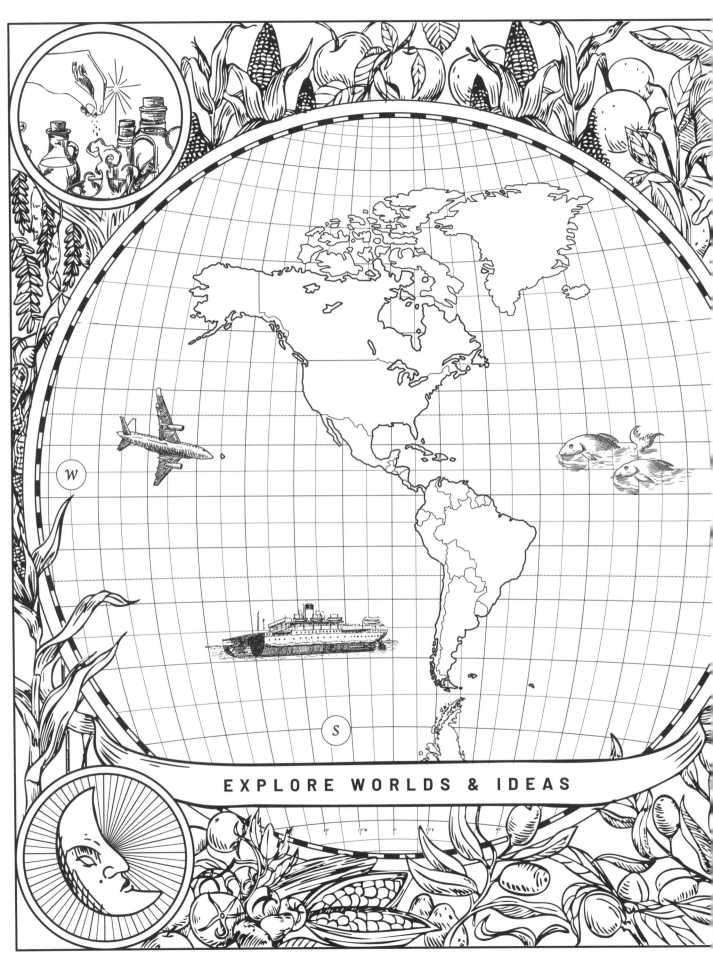

EXPLORE WORLDS & IDEAS

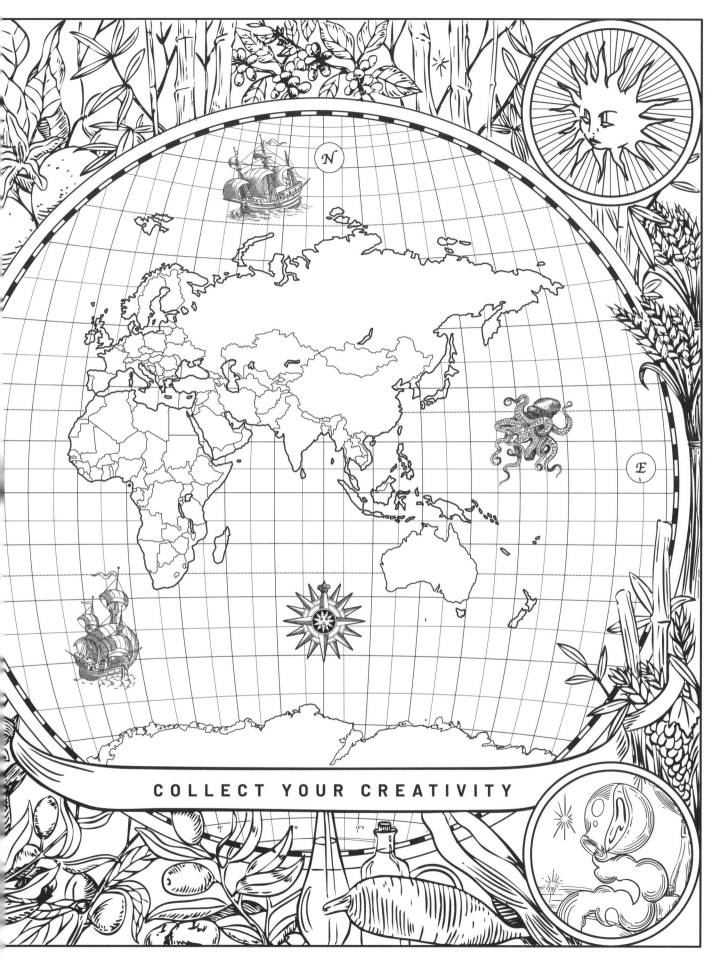

COLLECT YOUR CREATIVITY

INDEX

03	INTRODUCTION
06-13	INDEX
16-21	CONVERSION CHART
23	THE EXQUISITE FOUNDATION: GRAINS, NUTS, SEEDS, AND LEGUMES
24-39	GRAINS, NUTS, SEEDS, AND LEGUMES
40-43	BASIC PROCESSING TECHNIQUES FOR GRAINS, SEEDS NUTS, AND LEGUMES
45	POWDERS & FLOURS
46-47	TIPS ON HANDLING AND UTILIZING NUTS, GRAINS, SEEDS, AND LEGUMES
49-51	MESOAMERICAN PLANT-BASED CULINARY ALCHEMY
52-53	FOUNDATIONAL PROCESSES IN THE CONTEXT OF TIME
55-65	MOLES, MOJOS, TAPENADES, PICADAS, AND INFUSED OILS
66-67	YOUR DAILY BUTTER, BLEND & FORMULATE
68-69	PUMPKIN SEEDS
70-71	SUNFLOWER SEED
72-73	WATERMELON SEEDS
74-75	SESAME SEEDS
76-77	CASHEW NUTS
78-79	PEANUTS

80-81	ALMONDS
82	
83	
84	
85	
86	
87	
88	
89	
90	
91	
92	
93	
94	
95	
96	
97	
98	

INDEX

99

101   THE ART OF FERMENTATION: BRIDGING TRADITION AND INNOVATION

102-109   GLOBAL FUSION: EXPANDING THE FERMENTATION PALETTE

111-115   FERMENTED HOT SAUCES

117-129   ENHANCING FLAVORS & TEXTURES: ELABORATING FILLINGS & TOPPINGS

131   RECIPES AND NOTES

132

133

134

135

136

137

138

139

140

141

142

143

144	
145	
146	
147	
148	
149	
150	
151	
152	
153	
154	
155	
156	
157	
158	
159	
160	
161	

INDEX

162

163

164

165

166

167

168

169

170

171

172

173

174

175

176

177

178

179

180

181

182

183

184

185

186

187

188

189

190

191

192

193

194

195

196

197

INDEX

198

199

200

201

202

203

204

205

206

207

208

209

210

211

212

213

214

215

216	
217	
218	
219	
220	
221	
222	
223	
225-237	FROM FIELDS TO FEAST
238-239	BEVERAGE IDEAS
241-243	COCKTAIL SUGGESTIONS

CONVERSION CHARTS

CONVERSION CHARTS
VOLUME CONVERSIONS

FAHRENHEIT (°F)	CELSIUS (°C)	GAS MARK
225	107	1/4
250	121	1/2
275	135	1
300	149	2
325	163	3
350	177	4
375	191	5
400	204	6
425	218	7
450	232	8
475	246	9
500	260	10

A temperature conversion chart used in common oven temperatures for baking and roasting, between Fahrenheit, Celsius, and Gas Mark.

OVEN/STOVETOP TO
SLOW-COOKER CONVERSION CHART

TRADITIONAL COOKING TIME	SLOW COOKER ON LOW	SLOW COOKER ON HIGH
15-30 minutes	4-6 hours	1.5-2.5 hours
30-45 minutes	6-8 hours	3-4 hours
45 minutes to 3 hours	8-12 hours	4-6 hours

*TIPS FOR SLOW COOKING:

LOW TEMPERATURE:	Roughly equivalent to **190-200°F (88-93°C).**	
HIGH TEMPERATURE:	Roughly equivalent to **300-315°F (149-157°C).**	
LIQUIDS:	Because slow cookers have tightly sealed lids, the liquid doesn't evaporate as in traditional cooking. If adapting a recipe, you may need to reduce the liquid by about a third.	
VEGETABLES:	Root vegetables like carrots and potatoes cook slower than meat, so they should be placed at the bottom of the slow cooker.	

Remember, these are general guidelines. The exact conversion may vary based on the specific recipe and slow cooker model. Always check your slow cooker's manual for manufacturer's recommendations.

TEMPERATURE TECHNIQUES

Understanding and utilizing these temperature-based techniques enable chefs and home cooks to manipulate the cooking process, achieving desired textures and flavors while showcasing the art and science behind culinary practices. These nine culinary techniques showcase the profound impact of temperature and cooking duration on the texture, flavor, and overall quality of food.

High-temperature, short-duration methods like **flash-frying, stir-frying, searing,** and **grilling/broiling** (200°C to 290°C or 392°F to 550°F) quickly cook the exterior of the food. This rapid cooking creates crispy textures and rich, caramelized flavors through the Maillard reaction, while often keeping the interior tender and juicy.

Medium-temperature techniques such as **sautéing** and **roasting/baking** (around 180°C or 356°F) allow for more even cooking throughout the food. These methods balance the development of exterior flavors and textures with thorough interior cooking, making them ideal for a wide range of ingredients.

Low-temperature, long-duration methods like **steaming, sous-vide**, and **confit** (65°C to 100°C or 149°F to 212°F) gently cook food over extended periods. These techniques preserve moisture, nutrients, and delicate flavors, resulting in exceptionally tender and succulent dishes. **Steaming** cooks food using moist heat without leaching nutrients, **sous-vide** precisely controls temperature to achieve perfect doneness, and **confit** slowly cooks food in fat to enhance flavor and tenderness.

FLASH-FRYING: Cooking small or thin pieces of food at extremely high temperatures for a very short time. This technique results in a crispy exterior while keeping the interior tender. Example: making tempura.

STIR-FRYING: Quickly cooking bite-sized pieces of food in a wok over very high heat with constant stirring. This method preserves the texture and flavor of the ingredients.

SEARING: Applying high heat to the surface of food to create a caramelized crust, enhancing flavor and sealing in juices. Usually followed by further cooking at lower temperatures.

Grilling/Broiling: Cooking food using direct high heat from below (grilling) or above (broiling). This method imparts a smoky flavor and charred marks, cooking the food quickly.

SAUTÉING: Cooking food quickly in a small amount of oil or fat over medium-high heat. It's ideal for vegetables and thin cuts of meat, providing a browned exterior and tender interior.

ROASTING/BAKING: Using dry heat in an oven at moderate temperatures for a longer time. Suitable for larger cuts, and baked goods, it cooks the food evenly throughout.

STEAMING: Cooking food by surrounding it with steam in a confined space. This gentle method preserves nutrients and moisture, using lower temperatures than boiling.

SOUS-VIDE: Sealing food in airtight plastic bags and cooking it in a water bath at precisely controlled low temperatures for extended periods. This technique ensures even cooking and retains the food's moisture and flavor.

CONFIT: Slow-cooking food submerged in fat at very low temperatures over a long duration. It results in exceptionally tender and flavorful dishes.

TECHNIQUE	AVERAGE COOKING TEMPERATURE (°C)	AVERAGE COOKING TEMPERATURE (°F)
1. FLASH-FRYING	200°C	392°F
2. STIR-FRYING	220°C	428°F
3. SEARING	250°C	482°F
4. GRILLING/BROILING	290°C	550°F
5. SAUTÉING	180°C	356°F
6. ROASTING/BAKING	180°C	356°F
7. STEAMING	100°C	212°F
8. SOUS-VIDE	65°C	149°F
9. CONFIT	90°C	194°F

GRAMS TO OUNCES
CONVERSION CHART

GRAMS (G)	OUNCES (OZ)	GRAMS (G)	OUNCES (OZ)
5	0.18	450	15.87
10	0.35	500	17.64
20	0.71	550	19.40
30	1.06	600	21.16
40	1.41	650	22.93
50	1.76	700	24.69
100	3.53	750	26.46
150	5.29	800	28.22
200	7.05	850	29.98
250	8.82	900	31.75
300	10.58	950	33.51
350	12.35	1000	35.27
400	14.11		

*Conversion Formula: To convert grams to ounces, multiply the number of grams by 0.03527396.

MILLILITERS TO FLUID OUNCES
CONVERSION CHART

MILLILITERS (ML)	FLUID OUNCES (FL OZ)	MILLILITERS (ML)	FLUID OUNCES (FL OZ)
5	0.17	450	15.22
10	0.34	500	16.91
20	0.68	550	18.60
30	1.01	600	20.29
40	1.35	650	21.98
50	1.69	700	23.67
100	3.38	750	25.36
150	5.07	800	27.05
200	6.76	850	28.74
250	8.45	900	30.43
300	10.14	950	32.12
350	11.83	1000	33.81
400	13.53		

Conversion Formula: To convert milliliters to fluid ounces, multiply the number of milliliters by 0.033814.

THE EXQUISITE FOUNDATION:
GRAINS, NUTS, SEEDS, AND LEGUMES

Grains, nuts, seeds, and legumes form the bedrock of a nutritious and flavorful diet, each bringing its unique essence to your table. Though they may share some overlapping culinary uses and nutritional benefits, they stand apart in their botanical classifications and distinct roles within the plant kingdom. Understanding these differences not only deepens our appreciation for these exquisite ingredients but also empowers us to unlock their full potential in our diets and recipes.

These foundational foods are more than just simple ingredients; they are the building blocks of a healthy, vibrant life. Rich in nutrients and bursting with diverse flavors and textures, they offer endless culinary possibilities that can elevate any dish. By exploring their unique characteristics and benefits, we can maximize their contribution to our well-being and culinary enjoyment, transforming everyday meals into nourishing gastronomic experiences.

To deepen the incorporation of fusion into these notions, we can build upon the foundational elements of grains, nuts, seeds, and legumes by embracing the transformative potential of culinary fusion. In today's kitchen, blending ingredients and techniques from diverse culinary traditions allows us to reimagine classic recipes and innovate in exciting new ways.

By pairing Mesoamerican staples like amaranth or corn with unexpected global flavors such as Mediterranean herbs, Asian spices, or African seeds, we create a dialogue between ancient traditions and contemporary gastronomic trends. This fusion of cultures on the plate not only broadens our flavor horizons but also honors the rich heritage of the ingredients, reminding us that the act of cooking is an amalgam of cultures.

GRAINS, NUTS, SEEDS, AND LEGUMES

CATEGORY	DEFINITION	CULINARY USES	NUTRITIONAL PROFILE
SEEDS	Reproductive units of plants capable of developing into another plant. Can be from flowers, fruits, or vegetables.	You can eat it raw, roast it, grind it into flour, or make it into oils. It is also used in various dishes for texture and nutrition.	Generally rich in healthy fats, vitamins, minerals, and fiber. Some, like chia and flax seeds, are also high in omega-3 fatty acids.
NUTS	Botanically, a fruit is composed of a hard shell and a seed, where the hard-shelled fruit does not open to release the seed. Culinary nuts include many seeds.	You can eat it raw or roasted, use it in cooking and baking, or make it into butter and oils. It is common in desserts, salads, and vegetarian diets.	High in healthy monounsaturated and polyunsaturated fats, protein, fiber, vitamins, and minerals. Energy-dense.
GRAINS	Edible seeds of grasses belonging to the cereal family. Examples include wheat, rice, oats, barley, corn, and rye.	Used whole, ground into flour for bread and pasta, or processed into products like cereal and oatmeal. Staple foods globally.	Primary sources of carbohydrates provide protein, fiber, and various vitamins and minerals, especially in the whole form.
LEGUMES	Class of vegetables from plants in the Fabaceae family, including beans, lentils, peas, and peanuts (botanically a legume, not a nut).	Used in soups, stews, salads, and as meat substitutes. Can be eaten whole, pureed into spreads, or ground into flours.	Rich in protein, dietary fiber, vitamins, and minerals, and low in fat. The vital protein source in plant-based diets.

NUTRITIONAL BENEFITS

- **BALANCED DIET:** Grains, nuts, seeds, and legumes are rich in essential nutrients, including fiber, protein, healthy fats, vitamins, and minerals. Integrating these into meals contributes to a balanced diet, supporting overall health.

- **WEIGHT MANAGEMENT:** High in fiber and protein, these foods can increase satiety, helping to control appetite and support weight management efforts.

ENVIRONMENTAL IMPACT

- **SUSTAINABILITY:** Grains, legumes, and seeds, in particular, have a lower environmental footprint compared to animal-based proteins. By incorporating more of these plant-based ingredients into meals, households can contribute to reduced water usage, greenhouse gas emissions, and land use.

- **BIODIVERSITY:** Diversifying diets with various grains, nuts, seeds, and legumes can encourage agricultural diversity, support soil health, and reduce dependency on monoculture farming practices.

CULINARY DIVERSITY AND ENJOYMENT

- **FLAVOR AND TEXTURE:** These ingredients offer an array of flavors and textures, from the creaminess of nuts to the crunch of seeds and the heartiness of legumes. They can elevate the sensory experience of meals, making everyday dishes more exciting and enjoyable.

- **CULTURAL EXPLORATION:** Many grains, nuts, seeds, and legumes are staples in cuisines worldwide. Using them in home cooking can be a way to explore and celebrate global culinary traditions, introducing new recipes and cooking techniques.

- **CREATIVITY IN THE KITCHEN:** With such versatile ingredients, home cooks can experiment with new combinations and recipes, from grain bowls and nut-based sauces to seed toppings and legume-based mains. This not only adds variety to the diet but also fosters creativity and skill development in the kitchen.

ECONOMIC BENEFITS

- **COST-EFFECTIVENESS:** Many grains, legumes, and seeds are economical, especially when purchased in bulk. They can serve as the basis for nutritious, low-cost meals, reducing the grocery bill without compromising nutrition or taste.

SOCIAL AND FAMILY DYNAMICS

- **SHARED MEALS:** Cooking with these ingredients can be a shared activity, promoting family bonding and education about nutrition and culinary skills. Meals become an opportunity for connection and learning.

HEALTH AWARENESS: Integrating these foods into family meals can also educate household members about healthy eating habits, fostering a culture of wellness and preventive care through diet.

MOST ACCESSIBLE GRAINS, NUTS, SEEDS AND LEGUMES TABLE

LEGUMES

CHICKPEAS (GARBANZO BEANS)	Are rich in protein and are used in dishes like hummus and chana masala.	**PEAS**	Including green peas, split peas, and black-eyed peas, versatile in many dishes
LENTILS	Come in various colors, including red, brown, and green, and are high in protein and fiber.	**NAVY BEANS**	Small, white beans often used in soups, stews, and baked beans.
PEANUTS	Technically, they are legumes used in various culinary applications, from snacks to peanut butter.	**PINTO BEANS**	Commonly used in Mexican cuisine, good for refried beans.
KIDNEY BEANS	Popular in chili and salads, they must be cooked properly to eliminate toxins.	**LIMA BEANS**	Also known as butter beans, they are large and buttery in texture.
SOYBEANS	These are used to make tofu, tempeh, and soy milk, and they are high in protein.	**ADZUKI BEANS**	Small, red beans often used in Asian desserts.

LEGUMES

FAVA BEANS	Large green beans with a distinct flavor in Mediterranean cuisine.	**CHANA DAL (SPLIT CHICKPEAS)**	Used in Indian cuisine, similar to yellow split peas but with a sweeter taste.
CANNELLINI BEANS	White Italian beans, great in salads and soups.	**FRENCH GREEN LENTILS (PUY LENTILS)**	They taste peppery and are good for salads and side dishes.
RED LENTILS	Quick-cooking lentils, excellent for soups and Indian dal.	**CRANBERRY BEANS**	Streaked with red, creamy texture, used in Italian and Portuguese cuisine.
BLACK LENTILS (BELUGA LENTILS)	Hold their shape well and are suitable for salads and sides.	**BROAD BEANS (FAVA BEANS)**	Large beans are often removed from their outer pod and inner shell before eating.
EDAMAME	Young soybeans, served steamed with salt.	**BLACK BEANS**	A staple in Latin American cuisine, an excellent source of antioxidants.

LEGUMES

MUNG BEANS   Used in Asian cooking, sprouted for salads or cooked in dishes.

GREEN LENTILS   Retain their shape when cooked, which is ideal for salads.

SEEDS

CHIA SEEDS	Are rich in omega-3 fatty acids, fiber, and calcium.	**POPPY SEEDS**	Are rich in calcium, phosphorus, and iron.
FLAXSEEDS	Are high in omega-3 fatty acids and fiber and benefit heart health.	**QUINOA**	Though often cooked as a grain, quinoa is technically a seed. It is rich in protein, fiber, and all nine essential amino acids.
SESAME SEEDS	A good source of healthy fats, protein, B vitamins, minerals, fiber, and antioxidants.	**AMARANTH**	Another pseudocereal that's a complete protein; also high in iron, magnesium, and manganese.
PUMPKIN SEEDS (PEPITAS)	Packed with magnesium, zinc, and fatty acids.	**POMEGRANATE SEEDS**	Loaded with fiber, vitamins, and minerals and a great source of antioxidants.
HEMP SEEDS	Contain complete protein and a balanced ratio of omega-3 and omega-6 fatty acids.	**GRAPE SEEDS**	Often consumed as grape seed extract, known for their antioxidant properties.

SEEDS

MUSTARD SEEDS	Used in cooking and contain calcium, magnesium, and iron.	**SORGHUM**	Consumed like a grain but technically a seed; gluten-free and rich in antioxidants.
CORIANDER SEEDS	Offer dietary fiber, copper, zinc, and iron.	**CHARD SEEDS**	Though not commonly consumed, they can be sprouted or used in microgreen mixes.
CUMIN SEEDS	Good source of iron, promotes digestion and immunity.	**NIGELLA SEEDS (BLACK CUMIN)**	Have a distinct flavor and are packed with antioxidants.
FENNEL SEEDS	Are known for their antioxidant, anti-inflammatory, and antibacterial effects.	**TEFF**	A tiny seed rich in calcium, iron, and protein.
CARAWAY SEEDS	Rich in fiber, beneficial oils, and several essential minerals.	**BASIL SEEDS**	Are similar to chia seeds in their gel-forming property. They are high in fiber and have a cooling effect when consumed.

SEEDS

PINE NUTS   Are high in monounsaturated fats, iron, and magnesium.

SAFFLOWER SEEDS   These are used for their oil and are high in monounsaturated fats.

SUNFLOWER SEEDS   High in vitamin E, magnesium, and selenium.

NUTS

ALMONDS	Rich in Vitamin E, almonds are great for skin health.	**MACADAMIA NUTS**	High in healthy fats and low in carbs.
WALNUTS	Are high in omega-3 fatty acids, which support brain health.	**BRAZIL NUTS**	Best natural sources of selenium.
CASHEWS	A good source of magnesium and iron.	**PINE NUTS**	These are used in making pesto, and they're high in iron and magnesium.
PISTACHIOS	are lower in calories than many other nuts, but they're also rich in antioxidants.	**PEANUTS**	Loaded with fiber, vitamins, and minerals and a great source of antioxidants.
HAZELNUTS	High in fiber and Vitamin E.	**CHESTNUTS**	Are lower in fat than other nuts, and they're good sources of Vitamin C.

NUTS

TIGER NUTS	Not true nuts, but tubers are high in fiber.		**SACHA INCHI NUTS**	Also known as Inca peanuts, rich in omega-3, omega-6, and omega-9 fatty acids.
KOLA NUTS	Known for their caffeine content, they are used in some African cultures to flavor drinks.		**PEANUTS**	Loaded with fiber, vitamins, and minerals and a great source of antioxidants.
HICKORY NUTS	Native to North America, with a flavor similar to pecans.		**COCONUT**	While technically a fruit, its meat is often considered a nut. It is high in fiber and MCTs.
CANDLENUTS	Are a thickening agent in some Indonesian and Malaysian dishes, but they must be cooked before consumption.		**BUTTERNUTS**	Also known as white walnuts, butternuts offer a sweet, buttery flavor and are rich in oils and nutrients. Like walnuts, they can be used in baking and cooking.
BEECHNUTS	Small and triangular, used in some traditional European cuisines.		**BARU NUTS**	A recent addition to the superfood scene, high in protein and fiber.

NUTS

ACORNS   Edible after processing to remove
                 tannins, used in traditional dishes.

GINKGO NUTS Used in East Asian cuisine, must be
                 cooked and consumed in moderation.

PECANS   Contain more than 19 vitamins and
                 minerals.

ALMONDS   Versatile and nutritious, excellent for
                 heart health.

GRAINS

WHEAT	One of the world's most commonly consumed grains, used in bread, pasta, and many baked goods.		**SPELT**	An ancient wheat variety known for its nutty flavor, used in bread, pasta, and cereals.
RICE	A staple food for more than half of the world's population, available in varieties like white, brown, jasmine, and basmati.		**MILLET**	A group of small-seeded gluten-free grains used in porridge, breads, and beers.
CORN (MAIZE)	Is widely consumed worldwide and is used in products like cornmeal, polenta, and tortillas.		**QUINOA**	A pseudocereal that's a complete protein used in salads, soups, and as a rice substitute.
OATS	Are known for their health benefits, including lowering cholesterol levels. They are used in oatmeal, granola, and baking.		**BUCKWHEAT**	Despite its name, it's gluten-free and used in noodles, pancakes, and porridge.
BARLEY	Rich in fiber, vitamins, and minerals, used in soups, stews, and beer brewing.		**AMARANTH**	Another pseudocereal, rich in proteins and minerals, used in salads, soups, and for popping.

GRAINS

TEFF	The world's smallest grain, high in protein and calcium, used in injera and porridges.	**DURUM WHEAT**	The hardest wheat variety, used to make semolina flour for pasta and couscous.
KAMUT (KHORASAN WHEAT)	An ancient grain known for its rich, nutty flavor, used in bread, pasta, and salads	**EMMER**	An ancient wheat type, also known as farro, used in bread and pasta.
BULGUR	Partially cooked cracked wheat, a staple in Middle Eastern cuisine, used in tabbouleh and pilafs.	**EMMER**	An ancient wheat type, also known as farro, used in bread and pasta.
WILD RICE	Not rice but the seed of an aquatic grass, known for its chewy texture and nutty flavor.		
EINKORN	The oldest wheat variety, known for its higher protein and lower gluten content.		

GRAINS

BASIC PROCESSING TECHNIQUES FOR GRAINS, SEEDS NUTS, AND LEGUMES

END PRODUCT	STEP 1	STEP 2	STEP 3
POWDERS	Heat Drying Dry roast (optional)	Cool to room temperature	Grind to a fine powder
FLOURS	Clean and optionally soak	Dry thoroughly or lightly roast	Mill into a fine flour
PASTES	Blanch (for nuts) or soak	Drain and rinse	Blend to a paste, adding water as necessary
BUTTER	Roast lightly	Cool slightly	Process in a food processor until smooth and creamy
OILS	Cold press (for oils) or roast	Grind or crush	Press or extract oil using an oil press or extractor

These are some basic processing steps to transform grains, nuts, seeds, and legumes into powders, flours, pastes, kinds of butter, and oils. Please note that the specific processes might vary slightly depending on the ingredient and the desired end product's texture. Remember that not all grains, seeds, nuts, and legumes behave the same way or yield the same result through these various processes; we recommend engaging in your research and experimentation.

These are best for seeds and grains. Roasting is optional but can enhance flavor. They are suitable for making powdered spices or instant mixes.

Applies to all categories. Soaking before drying can make the flour more digestible. The end product is used for baking and cooking.

Common for nuts and legumes. Soaking beforehand improves texture and digestibility. Pastes are often used in sauces and spreads.

Nuts and seeds are primarily used. Roasting before processing enhances the nutty flavor and aids in releasing oils, making the butter creamier.

Generally made from seeds and nuts. Cold pressing retains nutritional quality, but some oils are extracted using heat or chemical processes for higher yields.

PREPARATION	STEP 1	STEP 2	STEP 3
MASA OR DOUGH	Mix masa (nixtamalized corn flour) with water. Mix single ingredients or composed doughs with fluids.	Knead until the dough is smooth and pliable.	Let the dough rest before shaping and cooking as desired.
MOJO	Crush garlic with salt and other spices (e.g., cumin).	Mix with citrus juice (lime or orange) and olive oil.	Let the mixture marinate to blend the flavors.
PICADAS	Toast or fry the ingredients (nuts, seeds, bread).	Grind the toasted ingredients with garlic and spices.	Blend with a bit of liquid to form a thick sauce or paste.
MOLES	Roast and/or fry the ingredients (chiles, spices, nuts, chocolate).	Blend the ingredients into a smooth paste, adding some liquid if necessary.	Cook the paste in a pot, gradually adding more liquid and seasonings, simmering until thickened.
TAPENADES	Pit and chop olives, capers, and anchovies (if used).	Crush garlic and mix with the chopped ingredients.	Blend the mixture while slowly adding olive oil to achieve a coarse paste consistency.

We also have outlined the basic steps for making Masa, Mojo, Picadas, Moles, and Tapenades. These culinary preparations vary greatly in their ingredients and techniques, reflecting diverse culinary applications in traditional or contemporary cuisine; we invite you to use these notions as a departing point in your explorations.

NOTES

Masa is a dough made from nixtamalized corn and is the base for many Mexican and Central American dishes, such as tortillas and tamales.

Mojo refers to various sauces, but commonly a Cuban garlic-citrus sauce is used as a marinade for meats and as a dressing.

Picadas are a foundational ingredient in many Spanish and Latin American dishes, providing depth and richness.

Moles encompass a variety of rich sauces integral to Mexican cuisine. They are known for their complexity and depth of flavor, often involving chocolate, chiles, and spices.

Tapenades are olive paste made to be spread or added as components in marinades. They are from the Provence region in France and typically contain olives, capers, anchovies, and olive oil. *Anchovies can easily be replaced with pickled mushrooms for a full-on plant-based recipe.*

POWDERS & FLOURS

The terms "powder" and "flour" in the context of plant-based edibles refer to the texture and intended use of the ground product. While they might seem similar, being both fine, dry substances derived from grinding grains, nuts, seeds, legumes, or other plant materials, there are subtle differences in their characteristics and applications. In summary, the main differences between powders and flours in plant-based edibles are their texture, source materials, and specific applications in cooking and baking. Powders are often used for their concentrated flavors, colors, or nutritional properties, while flours are essential for providing structure and texture to various dishes.

POWDER

- **TEXTURE AND FINENESS:** Powders are usually finer than flour and may feel silky or fine. The process aims to create a product with a uniform, ultra-fine consistency.

- **COMPOSITION:** Powders can be made from a wider variety of plant-based sources, including leaves (such as matcha from green tea leaves), roots (like turmeric), fruits (such as berry powders), and even certain vegetables.

- **USES:** Powders are often used for their flavor, color, or nutritional benefits and can be added to smoothies, juices, sauces, and baking recipes. They are also used as supplements, decoration, thickening agents, and/or coloring agents in foods.

- **EXAMPLES:** Cocoa powder, matcha powder, turmeric powder, and vegetable powders like spinach or beetroot powder.

FLOUR

TEXTURE AND FINENESS: Flours tend to have a slightly coarser texture than powders but are still delicate enough for baking and cooking. The grinding process focuses on creating a product that can structure baked goods.

COMPOSITION: Flours are primarily made from grains, nuts, seeds, and legumes. The choice of source material is often dictated by the need for a binding or structural component in recipes, particularly baking.

USE: Flours are integral in baking and cooking, functioning as the base for breads, pastries, cakes, and other dishes. They provide structure and texture, work as thickening agents, and yield bulk, influencing the final product's moisture content and density.

EXAMPLES: Wheat flour, almond flour, coconut flour, chickpea flour, and rice flour.

TIPS ON HANDLING AND UTILIZING NUTS, GRAINS, SEEDS, AND LEGUMES

STORING GRAINS

KEEP DRY AND COOL: Store grains in airtight containers in a cool, dry place to prevent them from absorbing moisture and odors. This also helps deter pests.

REFRIGERATION FOR WHOLE GRAINS: Whole grains contain oils that can go rancid. Consider refrigerating or freezing them to extend their shelf life.

PREPARING LEGUMES

SOAKING: Soak beans and legumes overnight to reduce cooking time and make them more digestible by reducing phytic acid and lectins. Dispose of and change the water before cooking.

QUICK SOAK METHOD: If you're short on time, boil the legumes for a few minutes and let them soak for an hour off the heat.

RINSE BEFORE COOKING: Always rinse legumes thoroughly before cooking to remove dirt or debris.

UTILIZING SEEDS

TOASTING FOR FLAVOR: Toast seeds like sesame, sunflower, and pumpkin in a dry pan over medium heat or in the oven to enhance their nutty flavor. Watch closely to avoid burning.

GROUND SEEDS FOR ABSORPTION: Grinding flax seeds and chia seeds can help your body absorb their nutrients more efficiently.

COOKING WITH NUTS

ROASTING TO ENHANCE FLAVOR: Roast nuts in the oven or stove to deepen their flavor. This can be done with or without oil and spices.

SKIN REMOVAL: Some recipes may call for skinned nuts. Blanch almonds and hazelnuts in boiling water for a minute, then cool them in icy water to easily remove the skins.

PREPARING LEGUMES

ROTATION: Rotate your stock of nuts, grains, seeds, and legumes. Use older items first and restock with fresh supplies to ensure quality.

CHECK FOR FRESHNESS: Periodically check your stock for signs of spoilage, such as mold or unusual odors, especially if it is not stored in the freezer or fridge.

PORTION AND FREEZE: For items you use less frequently, consider storing them in smaller portions. This way, you can thaw only what you need, keeping the rest fresh.

BULK BUYING: While buying in bulk can save money, consider your consumption rate. It's only economical if you can store them properly and use them before they spoil.

Adopting these practices can help you maximize the shelf life, flavor, and nutritional value of nuts, grains, seeds, and legumes in your kitchen.

MESOAMERICAN PLANT-BASED CULINARY ALCHEMY

Welcome to "Mesoamerican Plant-Based Culinary Alchemy," where the ancient wisdom of Mesoamerica intertwines with the transformative essence of the seed, guiding us on a mesmerizing journey into plant-based cuisine.

Within these pages, we offer you a portal to the past, one reimagined through the lens of modern culinary innovation. Here, grains, nuts, seeds, and legumes are not merely ingredients—they are sacred elements imbued with the potential to weave a tapestry of flavors as rich and diverse as the cultures of Mesoamerica.

By exploring the alchemy of these ingredients and processes, we invite you to transcend the ordinary, transforming humble plant-based staples into culinary wonders. Enter the heart of Mesoamerican culinary traditions, where each recipe is a testament to nature's enduring bounty and the creative spirit that brings it to life.

Join us on this journey of experimentation and discovery, where tradition meets creativity, and ancient knowledge gives rise to contemporary plant-powered cuisine. "Mesoamerican Plant-Based Culinary Alchemy" is more than a guide—it is your companion in the enchanting world of culinary transformation.

MESOAMERICAN PLANT-BASED CULINARY ALCHEMY

ANCESTRAL & CONTEMPORARY ALCHEMY

At the heart of ancestral alchemy is the profound relationship between Mesoamerican cultures and their natural environment. Ingredients such as maize, beans, squash, chili peppers, cacao, and vanilla form the cornerstone of traditional recipes. Techniques like nixtamalization—where maize is soaked and cooked in an alkaline solution, typically lime water, then hulled—exemplify the ancient wisdom that enhances both the nutritional value and digestibility of food.

Another critical element is the use of metates (stone grinding tools) and molcajetes (stone mortars), which are employed to grind and blend spices, seeds, and grains. These imbue dishes with distinctive textures and flavors impossible to replicate with modern machinery.

Contemporary alchemy in the Mesoamerican kitchen is characterized by an adventurous spirit that experiments with new techniques and global influences while staying rooted in tradition. Modern chefs and home cooks are reinterpreting age-old dishes through the lens of current culinary trends, dietary preferences, and sustainability concerns.

For example, the incorporation of plant-based proteins to reinterpret traditional dishes for vegan and vegetarian diets showcases how contemporary needs are met with innovative solutions. Techniques like sous-vide cooking, fermentation, and molecular gastronomy are applied to traditional ingredients, creating exciting textures and flavors that bridge the old with the new.

FUSION AND GLOBAL INFLUENCE

The global exchange of culinary ideas has introduced Mesoamerican flavors to the world and vice versa. Ingredients from other cuisines are embraced and woven into Mesoamerican dishes, creating fusion foods that still honor traditional essence. For instance, introducing Middle Eastern or Asian spices into Mesoamerican dishes introduces new flavors while respecting the cuisine's foundational elements.

SUSTAINABLE PRACTICES

Sustainability is another crucial aspect of the contemporary Mesoamerican kitchen, reflecting a return to ancestral respect for the land. This includes the revival of heirloom crops, the promotion of biodiversity, and the practice of permaculture in food production. Chefs and food producers increasingly source ingredients locally and seasonally, supporting small farmers and indigenous communities, thus ensuring that culinary traditions are preserved for future generations.

THE ROLE OF TECHNOLOGY

Technology plays a significant role in contemporary culinary practices, from the way recipes are shared and learned through social media and cooking apps to the use of high-tech kitchen equipment that allows for precision cooking. This accessibility and innovation make Mesoamerican cuisine more dynamic and far-reaching than ever before.

In summary, the blend of ancestral wisdom and contemporary innovation in today's Mesoamerican kitchen is a powerful testament to the region's rich culinary legacy and its adaptive, forward-thinking approach to food. This alchemy not only preserves the past but also ensures that Mesoamerican cuisine continues to evolve and inspire, both locally and globally.

FOUNDATIONAL PROCESSES IN THE CONTEXT OF TIME

ANCIENT: Cacao powder was used in beverages and ceremonial foods.

MODERN: Spirulina and chlorella powders are added to smoothies and dishes to boost nutrients and vibrant colors.

ANCIENT: Chia and flax seeds for thickening and adding texture to beverages and puddings.

MODERN: Seeds are now superfoods sprinkled on dishes for added nutrients or used to create plant-based egg substitutes in baking.

(MOLES, MOJOS, PICADAS & TAPENADES)

ANCIENT: Complex moles combining dozens of spices, chilies, and chocolate.

MODERN: Incorporation of global spices and umami-rich ingredients like miso and soy sauce to create innovative moles.

ANCIENT: Beans and lentils as staple protein sources in soups, stews, and fillings.

MODERN: Lentil and bean flour for high-protein, gluten-free cooking and baking alternatives.

POWDERS

SEEDS

PASTES

LEGUMES

GRAINS

FLOUR

NUTS

KINDS OF BUTTER

ANCIENT: Maize, the cornerstone of Mesoamerican cuisine, is used in many traditional dishes.

MODERN: Ancient grains like teff and spelt are revived for their nutritional profiles and sustainability, used in artisan bread and modern recipes.

ANCIENT: Nixtamalized corn flour for tortillas and tamales.

MODERN: Quinoa and amaranth flours for gluten-free baking, enriching dishes with protein and amino acids.

ANCIENT: Nuts like pecans and pine nuts used in traditional dishes and confections.

MODERN: Nuts are now also milked, creating dairy-free beverages and creams, expanding their use in plant-based and lactose-intolerant diets.

ANCIENT: Ground pumpkin seed butter used in sauces and soups.

MODERN: Nut butter, such as almonds and cashews, is a creamy base for plant-based dishes and desserts.

MOLES, MOJOS, TAPENADES, PICADAS, AND INFUSED OILS

Pastes and infused oils are potent flavor enhancers that are the foundation for many dishes, delivering intense and concentrated tastes that elevate any recipe. In this culinary companion, we introduce you to the world of moles, mojos, tapenades, picadas, and infused oils—each a testament to the rich culinary traditions of Mesoamerican cuisine while also serving as a gateway to innovative, modern flavor combinations.

These preparations not only pay homage to the deep, complex heritage of Mesoamerican and Mediterranean cuisines but also adapt and evolve these traditions for contemporary palates. Whether crafting a traditional dish or experimenting with new culinary creations, these flavor-packed components provide versatility and depth. They can be used as marinades, spreads, sauces, or finishing touches, transforming everyday ingredients into extraordinary meals.

By incorporating these powerful preparations into your culinary repertoire, you will craft a versatile atlas of ingredients and techniques to transform your meals into flavorful, memorable experiences. Whether used as a base, dressing, spread, marinade, or finishing touch, these flavor bombs will help you push the boundaries of traditional cuisine while respecting and celebrating its origins.

MOLES

Moles are rich, complex sauces integral to Mexican cuisine. They feature an intricate blend of spices, chiles, nuts, seeds, and often chocolate. Each region in Mexico boasts its variant, making mole a symbol of cultural and culinary diversity.

Applications: Traditionally served over poultry, mole is versatile enough to accompany a wide range of animal or plant-based meats. In contemporary cuisine, mole can be used as a base for stews, as a sauce for enchiladas, or as a flavoring agent in innovative dishes like mole-infused chocolates or mole pizza, showcasing its adaptability across various culinary platforms.

CLASSIC MOLE POBLANO:

Blending ancho, pasilla, and mulato chiles with dark chocolate and spices.

MOLE VERDE:

Featuring pumpkin seeds, green tomatoes, and jalapeño peppers for a fresh, herby flavor.

MOLE AMARILLO:

Utilizing yellow guajillo chiles, roasted garlic, and cumin for a vibrant, earthy taste.

PISTACHIO MOLE:

Ancho chili sauce;
Ancho-spiced chocolate

MOLE NEGRO:

Combining black chiles, chocolate, and a mix of nuts, including almonds and pecans for depth.

MOLE ROJO:

Highlighting red chiles, peanuts, and sesame seeds, with a touch of cinnamon.

ALMOND MOLE:

A creamy variation with blanched almonds, white chocolate, and ancho chiles.

MOLE DE CAFÉ:

Infusing traditional mole ingredients with coffee grounds for a unique, bitter twist.

FRUIT MOLE:

Integrating dried fruits like apricots and raisins into the sauce for a sweet-savory profile.

MOJOS

Mojos are flavorful sauces originating from Spanish cuisine. They are characterized by garlic, olive oil, citrus, or vinegar, alongside herbs and spices. Mojos serve as lively accents to dishes, bringing brightness and zest.

Applications: Mojos are traditionally used as marinades for meats and seafood or as dipping sauces for bread and potatoes. In modern kitchens, mojos can dress salads, enhance grilled vegetables, or provide a vibrant drizzle for roasted meats, infusing them with a burst of flavor.

MOJOS DE AJO:

A garlic-heavy sauce with lime juice and cilantro, perfect for seafood.

MOJOS PICÓN:

This spicy sauce with red peppers, chili flakes, and paprika is ideal for drizzling over potatoes.

ORANGE CUMIN MOJO:

Featuring orange juice, cumin, and garlic for a citrusy kick.

AVOCADO MOJO:

Blending ripe avocado, cilantro, and green chiles for a creamy sauce.

TOMATO MOJO:

Using roasted tomatoes, garlic, and jalapeños for a versatile condiment.

MOJOS VERDE:

A green sauce with parsley, cilantro, and garlic enriched with olive oil.

MANGO MOJO:

Sweet and spicy with mango puree, habanero, and lime juice.

PEANUT MOJO:

A unique twist incorporating peanut butter, orange juice, and chipotle peppers.

TAMARIND MOJO:

A tangy and sweet sauce with tamarind paste, ginger, and honey.

TAPENADES

Originating from the Provence region in France, tapenades are thick, savory pastes made from finely chopped or blended olives, capers, anchovies, and olive oil. They often include additional ingredients like garlic, herbs, and lemon juice.

Applications: Beyond being a spread for crackers and bread, tapenades make excellent accompaniments to grilled meats, a flavorful base for sandwiches, or a robust addition to pasta and vegetable dishes. They can also be used to stuff poultry or fish, adding depth and richness to the cuisine.

CLASSIC OLIVE TAPENADE:

A blend of black olives, capers, and anchovies, with a touch of lemon zest.

SUN-DRIED TOMATO TAPENADE:

Combining sun-dried tomatoes, almonds, and basil for a Mediterranean flair.

CILANTRO JALAPEÑO TAPENADE:

A fresh mix of cilantro, pickled jalapeños, and pumpkin seeds.

MANGO BLACK BEAN TAPENADE:

Sweet mango paired with black beans, lime, and chili powder.

POBLANO ALMOND TAPENADE:

Roasted poblano peppers and toasted almonds with a hint of garlic.

CHIPOTLE CHERRY TAPENADE:

Smoky chipotle peppers with sweet cherries and walnuts.

ROASTED CORN TAPENADE:

Charred corn kernels with serrano peppers and cotija cheese.

CACAO NIB TAPENADE:

A sweet-savory blend of cacao nibs, olives, and pistachios.

PUMPKIN SEED TAPENADE:

Toasted pumpkin seeds, cilantro, and lime juice for a nutty spread.

PICADAS

In the context of Catalan cuisine, picadas are thickening and flavoring agents made by grinding together nuts, herbs, and other aromatics. They traditionally add body and complexity to stews, soups, and sauces.

Applications: Picadas can be used to enrich the flavor base of virtually any stew or soup, lending them a nuanced depth. They're also excellent for enhancing the sauces of braised dishes, whether meat, fish, or vegetables, and can be adapted to create innovative crusts for baked or roasted culinary creations.

ACHIOTE AND PUMPKIN SEED PICADA:

Ground pumpkin seeds and achiote paste, blended with garlic and olive oil, perfect for adding depth to vegetable and fish dishes.

CACAO AND CHILE PICADA:

A bold combination of roasted cacao nibs and dried chipotle chiles, ground with roasted almonds, to finish off rich meat stews.

AVOCADO LEAF AND TOASTED CORN PICADA:

Dried avocado leaves and toasted corn kernels ground with garlic and sea salt, ideal for thickening and scenting sauces for chicken or turkey.

TOMATILLO AND PEPITA PICADA:

Roasted tomatillos and pumpkin seeds, crushed with cilantro and serrano peppers, adding a zesty finish to seafood or pork.

CILANTRO SEED AND LIME ZEST PICADA:

Ground cilantro (coriander) seeds and lime zest, mixed with crushed peanuts, to sprinkle over grilled vegetables or fish for a fresh, aromatic lift.

COFFEE AND BLACK BEAN PICADA:

Finely ground coffee beans and black beans mixed with toasted walnuts and a hint of chipotle make this dish perfect for complementing beef dishes.

MANGO AND HABANERO PICADA:

Dried mango and habanero peppers, ground with roasted cashews, to add a sweet-heat twist to chicken or shrimp.

HIBISCUS AND ALMOND PICADA:

Dried hibiscus flowers and blanched almonds, ground with a touch of garlic, ideal for enriching lamb or duck sauces with a floral note.

TAMARIND AND MACADAMIA PICADA:

Sour tamarind paste and roasted macadamia nuts, combined with a hint of raw sugar, to finish sauces for fish or pork with a tangy, nutty flavor.

INFUSED OILS

Infused oils are made by steeping herbs, spices, fruits, or other flavoring agents in oil, allowing the oil to absorb their flavors over time. This process creates a versatile ingredient that can carry the essence of the infusing elements.

Applications: Infused oils can be used in many ways - as a finishing oil for dishes to add flavor, in salad dressings, for sautéing, or even in baking to introduce subtle nuances to the food. They're particularly effective in drizzling over grilled bread, enhancing pasta dishes, or elevating the taste profile of grilled meats and vegetables.

GARLIC CILANTRO OIL:

Infused with roasted garlic and fresh cilantro for a fragrant touch.

CHIPOTLE OLIVE OIL:

Smoky chipotle peppers lend a spicy depth to olive oil.

LIME AVOCADO OIL:

Zesty lime zest infused in avocado oil, perfect for dressings.

CUMIN SEED OIL:

Toasted cumin seeds give a warm, earthy flavor to vegetable oil.

HERB INFUSED OIL

A blend of rosemary, thyme, and oregano in olive oil for a Mediterranean twist.

CHILI LIME OIL:

Spicy chili flakes and lime zest for a tangy and hot oil.

VANILLA BEAN COCONUT OIL:

Sweet vanilla beans are infused in coconut oil, which is ideal for baking.

CACAO NIB OIL:

Roasted cacao nibs create a subtly sweet and chocolatey oil.

COFFEE BEAN OIL:

Coffee beans steeped in oil for a rich, aromatic infusion.

YOUR DAILY BUTTER, BLEND & FORMULATE

Nut and seed butter are not only powerhouses of energy and nutrition, but they also bring a depth of flavor and texture that can transform everyday meals. These versatile spreads are rich in healthy fats, proteins, and essential nutrients, making them an indispensable staple in the modern kitchen. Whether inspired by the ancient culinary traditions of Mesoamerican and Latino cuisines or contemporary culinary innovation, nut and seed butter can elevate your dishes in countless ways.

BLEND & FORMULATE: NUT & SEED BUTTER

Use them as a hearty spread on toast, a creamy base for sauces, or a flavorful ingredient in baking and cooking. Their unique characteristics shine through whether you're blending them into smoothies, stirring them into oatmeal, or incorporating them into savory dishes. How you process nuts and seeds—whether through blanching, drying, or roasting—can dramatically alter their flavor profiles and textures, from the smooth richness of roasted almond butter to the delicate nuttiness of raw cashew butter. We encourage you to experiment with different combinations from our kitchen to enhance your culinary experience, exploring the full potential of these everyday staples.

TIPS FOR MAKING DELICIOUS BUTTER

For making your own seed and nut butter, several key considerations ensure the final product is flavorful, high-quality, and safe for consumption. Here are some essential factors we recommend you to keep in mind:

1. QUALITY OF INGREDIENTS
- **FRESHNESS:** Use fresh nuts and seeds, as they are the foundation of your butter and significantly affect flavor and texture.
- **VARIETY SELECTION:** Different nuts and seeds have unique flavors and oil contents. Choose varieties that match the desired outcome for your butter.

2. ROASTING
- **FLAVOR DEVELOPMENT:** Roasting can enhance the nutty flavors but requires careful monitoring to avoid burning, which can impart a bitter taste.
- **TEMPERATURE AND TIME:** Optimal roasting temperatures and times vary between types of nuts and seeds. Experimentation may be necessary to find the perfect balance.

3. PROCESSING
- **CONSISTENCY:** The processing time will affect the consistency of the butter, from crunchy to smooth. The desired texture will dictate the processing duration.
- **EQUIPMENT:** High-quality food processors or nut grinders ensure a smooth, consistent texture and can handle the oils released during grinding.

4. OIL SEPARATION

- **NATURAL PROCESS:** Oil separation is natural for homemade and natural nut butter without emulsifiers. Stirring before use is typically necessary.

- **PREVENTION:** Some producers add oils or fats that solidify at room temperature, like palm oil, to prevent separation. However, these additives may affect the product's health profile.

5. ADDITIVES

- **FLAVORS AND SWEETENERS:** Adding flavors (vanilla, chocolate, etc.) or sweeteners (honey, maple syrup, etc.) can enhance the product but may alter its nutritional profile.

- **SALT:** A small amount of salt can enhance the natural flavors of the nuts and seeds.

- **PRESERVATIVES:** Most natural nut butter does not contain preservatives, which limits their shelf life, but that is part of their appeal.

6. STORAGE

- **SHELF STABILITY:** Proper storage is critical for maintaining freshness. Nut butter can become rancid if exposed to heat, light, or air for prolonged periods.

- **REFRIGERATION:** Some nut butter, especially those without preservatives, require refrigeration after opening to extend their shelf life.

7. NUTRITIONAL VALUE

- **HEALTH BENEFITS:** Nuts and seeds contain healthy fats, proteins, vitamins, and minerals.

- **ALLERGENS:** Clearly label any common allergens, as nut allergies are prevalent and can be severe.

8. PACKAGING

- **AIR-TIGHT CONTAINERS:** Packaging should protect the product from air and light to maintain freshness.

- **LABELING:** Include nutritional information, ingredients, best before dates.

PUMPKIN SEED PANELA

ADDITIONAL INGREDIENTS
Panela, Sea Salt, Organic Cold-Pressed Pumpkin Seed Oil

FLAVOR DESCRIPTION
A sweet and earthy spread with a caramel-like undertone from the panela, enhanced by the nuttiness of pumpkin seeds.

PUMPKIN HONEY

ADDITIONAL INGREDIENTS
Raw Honey, Cinnamon, Sea Salt

FLAVOR DESCRIPTION
Sweet and comforting with a hint of spice, perfect for drizzling over morning toast or blending into smoothies.

**PUMPKIN
SEEDS**

PUMPKIN PEANUT

ADDITIONAL INGREDIENTS
Molasses, Chili Powder, Lime Zest, Sea Salt

FLAVOR DESCRIPTION
A bold blend of sweet and spicy, with a zesty kick that brings out the depth of peanuts and pumpkin seeds.

PUMPKIN MACADAMIA

ADDITIONAL INGREDIENTS
Maple Syrup, Nutmeg, Sea Salt

FLAVOR DESCRIPTION
Buttery and smooth with a sweet, nutty flavor profile, complemented by the warm spice of nutmeg.

SUNFLOWER SEED DARK CHOCOLATE

ADDITIONAL INGREDIENTS
Powdered Sugar, Organic Powder, Organic Cocoa Butter, Sea Salt

FLAVOR DESCRIPTION
Decadently rich with a smooth chocolate flavor, balanced by the slight saltiness and the robustness of sunflower seeds.

SUNFLOWER VANILLA

ADDITIONAL INGREDIENTS
Powdered Sugar, Vanilla Extract, Cinnamon, Nutmeg, Sea Salt

FLAVOR DESCRIPTION
Sweet and aromatic, with comforting vanilla and warm spices, offering a creamy and indulgent spread.

SUNFLOWER SEED

SUNFLOWER SEED BUTTER

ADDITIONAL INGREDIENTS
Cinnamon, vanilla extract, sea salt

FLAVOR DESCRIPTION
A sweet, aromatic spread with warm notes of cinnamon and vanilla, perfect for toast or fruit dipping.

SUNFLOWER SEED BUTTER & RASPBERRY

ADDITIONAL INGREDIENTS
Lemon zest, powdered sugar, a touch of balsamic vinegar

FLAVOR DESCRIPTION
A tangy, fruity spread with a balanced sweetness and slight tartness, ideal for pairing with pastries.

WATERMELON SEED

ADDITIONAL INGREDIENTS
Powdered Sugar, Expeller Pressed Sunflower Oil, Sea Salt

FLAVOR DESCRIPTION
This unique, lightly sweetened spread offers a fresh twist. Its distinct, nutty flavor is derived from watermelon seeds.

COCOA WATERMELON SEED BUTTER

ADDITIONAL INGREDIENTS
Unsweetened cocoa powder, maple syrup, vanilla extract

FLAVOR DESCRIPTION
A rich, chocolatey spread with a nutty undertone, perfect for desserts or as a spread on toast.

WATERMELON SEEDS

COCONUT-LIME WATERMELON SEED BUTTER

ADDITIONAL INGREDIENTS
Coconut flakes, lime zest, a touch of agave syrup

FLAVOR DESCRIPTION
This tropical, tangy spread combines the fresh flavor of lime with the richness of coconut. It's great for smoothies or as a dip.

CINNAMON-HONEY WATERMELON SEED BUTTER

ADDITIONAL INGREDIENTS
Ground cinnamon, honey, a pinch of sea salt

FLAVOR DESCRIPTION
A warm, spiced spread with a hint of sweetness and salt, ideal for pairing with fruit or as a toast topping.

SESAME-ALMOND BUTTER WITH HONEY

ADDITIONAL INGREDIENTS
Almonds, honey, sea salt

FLAVOR DESCRIPTION
A smooth and creamy blend of nutty sesame seeds and almonds, sweetened with honey for a rich, earthy, and slightly sweet flavor with a hint of salt.

BLACK SESAME SEED

ADDITIONAL INGREDIENTS
Honey, Sea Salt

FLAVOR DESCRIPTION
It is intensely nutty with an exquisite hint of sweetness, showcasing the rich, smoky flavor of black sesame.

SESAME SEEDS

SESAME-PUMPKIN SEED BUTTER WITH MAPLE SYRUP

ADDITIONAL INGREDIENTS
Pumpkin seeds, maple syrup, cinnamon, nutmeg

FLAVOR DESCRIPTION
A fall-inspired butter that blends the nuttiness of sesame seeds and pumpkin seeds with the warm sweetness of maple syrup and a touch of cinnamon and nutmeg, creating a cozy, spiced flavor.

TAHINI-CASHEW BUTTER WITH ZA'ATAR

ADDITIONAL INGREDIENTS
Cashews, Za'atar seasoning, lemon zest

FLAVOR DESCRIPTION
This Middle Eastern-inspired butter combines the nutty depth of tahini with creamy cashews, spiced with za'atar, and brightened with lemon zest, offering a savory and tangy flavor profile.

CASHEW ORANGE BLOSSOM HONEY

ADDITIONAL INGREDIENTS
Orange Blossom Honey, Orange Zest, Sea Salt

FLAVOR DESCRIPTION
Floral and fragrant, it is sweetened with orange blossom honey, adding a citrusy brightness to the creamy cashew base.

CASHEW ESPRESSO

ADDITIONAL INGREDIENTS
Coffee Beans, Maple Sugar, Vanilla, Sea Salt

FLAVOR DESCRIPTION
A caffeinated nut butter with robust coffee flavors, sweetened with maple sugar and a touch of vanilla.

CASHEW NUTS

CASHEW-PUMPKIN SEED BUTTER

ADDITIONAL INGREDIENTS
Pumpkin Seeds, Cinnamon, Honey, Sea Salt

FLAVOR DESCRIPTION
A slightly sweet and earthy spread, with the subtle spice of cinnamon and the toasty flavor of pumpkin seeds.

MAPLE-CASHEW ALMOND BUTTER

ADDITIONAL INGREDIENTS
Almonds, Maple Syrup, Vanilla Extract

FLAVOR DESCRIPTION
A rich and creamy blend with a sweet, nutty flavor enhanced by the warmth of maple syrup and vanilla.

PEANUT CHIPOTLE Y CHILES GUAQUES

ADDITIONAL INGREDIENTS
Chipotle Peppers, Chiles Guaques, Maple Sugar, Sea Salt

FLAVOR DESCRIPTION
Smoky and spicy with a touch of sweetness, capturing the essence of Mesoamerican flavors in a versatile spread.

PEANUT-ALMOND BUTTER BLEND

ADDITIONAL INGREDIENTS
Almond butter, honey, cinnamon, sea salt

FLAVOR DESCRIPTION
A smooth, nutty blend with a warm hint of cinnamon and a touch of sweetness, perfect for spreading on toast or using in desserts.

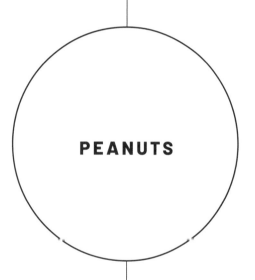

PEANUTS

PEANUT-CASHEW SEED BUTTER

ADDITIONAL INGREDIENTS
Cashew butter, chia seeds, maple syrup, vanilla extract

FLAVOR DESCRIPTION
Creamy and slightly sweet, with the added crunch of chia seeds and a hint of vanilla, it's great for smoothies or baking.

PEANUT-SESAME BUTTER FUSION

ADDITIONAL INGREDIENTS
Tahini (sesame paste), roasted sunflower seeds, honey

FLAVOR DESCRIPTION
A rich, earthy combination with a balance of nutty flavors from sesame and sunflower seeds, ideal for savory dishes or as a dip.

ALMOND DARK CHOCOLATE

ADDITIONAL INGREDIENTS
Cocoa Powder, Powdered Sugar, Sea Salt

FLAVOR DESCRIPTION
Smooth and rich, it combines the natural sweetness of almonds with the indulgence of dark chocolate for a luxurious treat.

ALMOND-CASHEW BUTTER WITH CARDAMOM

ADDITIONAL INGREDIENTS
Cashews, cardamom, honey, sea salt

FLAVOR DESCRIPTION
A creamy, slightly sweet butter with a warm, aromatic flavor profile inspired by Middle Eastern cuisine.

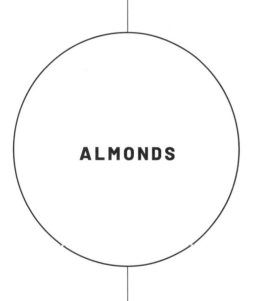

ALMONDS

ALMOND-PISTACHIO BUTTER WITH ROSE

ADDITIONAL INGREDIENTS
Pistachios, rose water, maple syrup, sea salt

FLAVOR DESCRIPTION
A delicately floral and nutty spread with a hint of sweetness, evoking the flavors of Persian desserts.

ALMOND-SESAME BUTTER WITH MISO

ADDITIONAL INGREDIENTS
Sesame seeds (tahini), white miso paste, honey, soy sauce

FLAVOR DESCRIPTION
A savory and umami-rich butter with a slight sweetness, blending the nuttiness of almonds with Asian flavors.

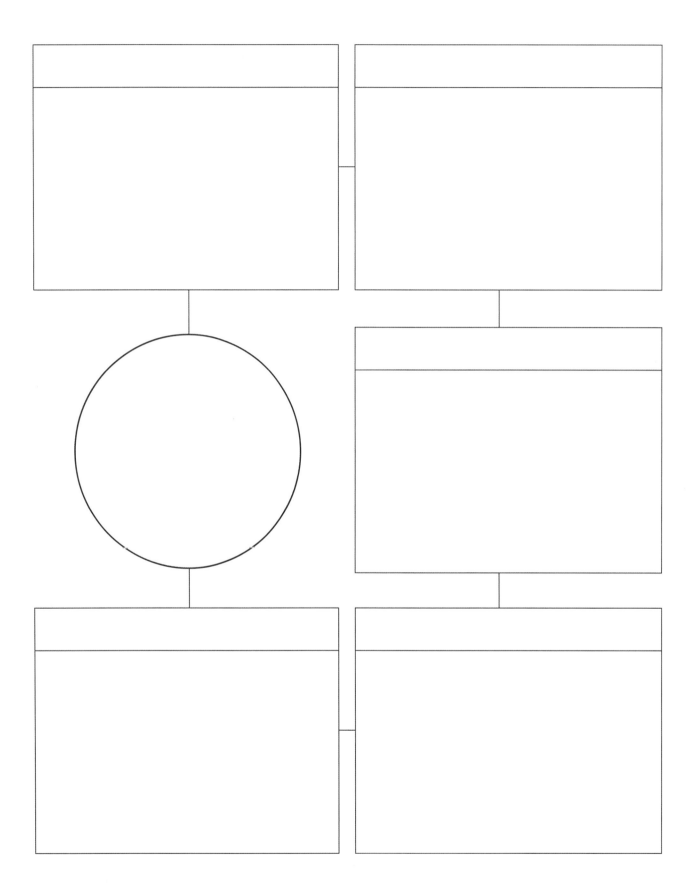

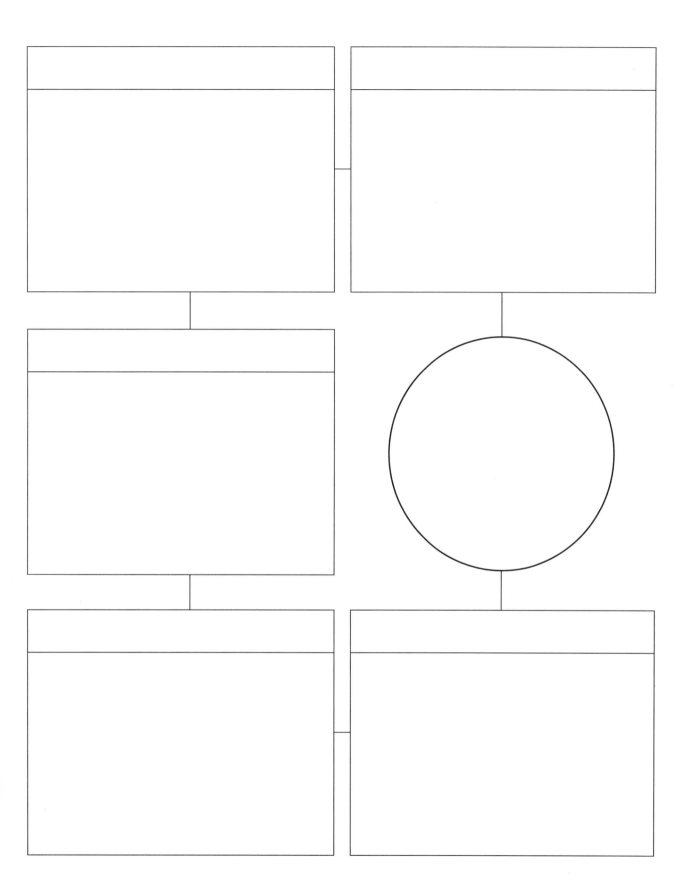

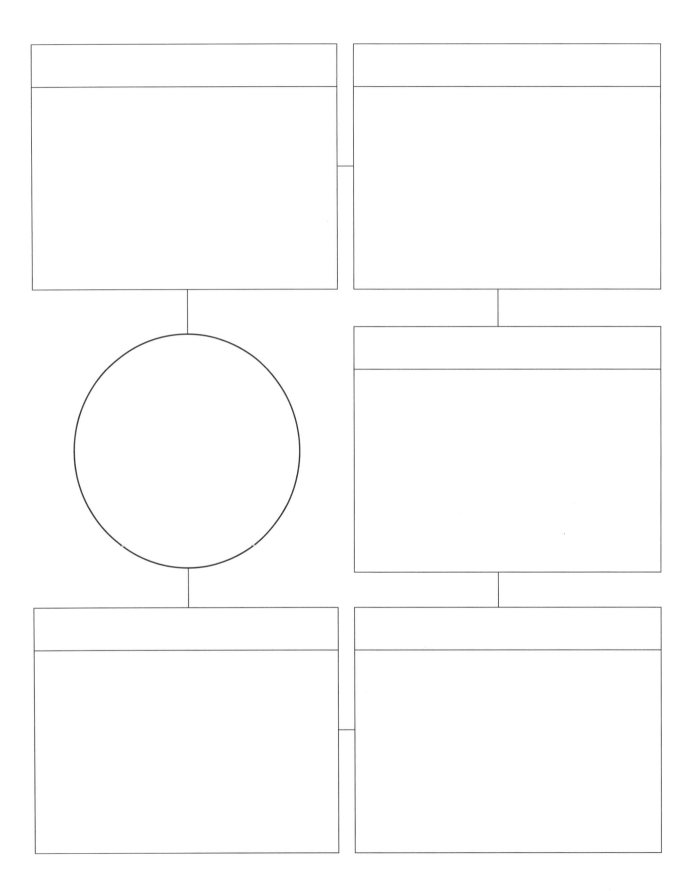

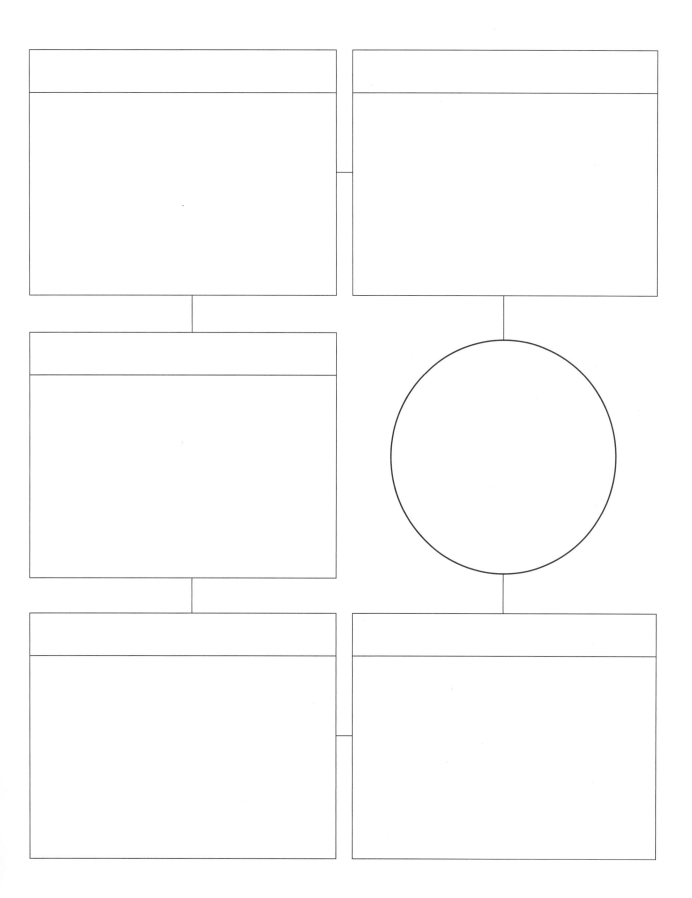

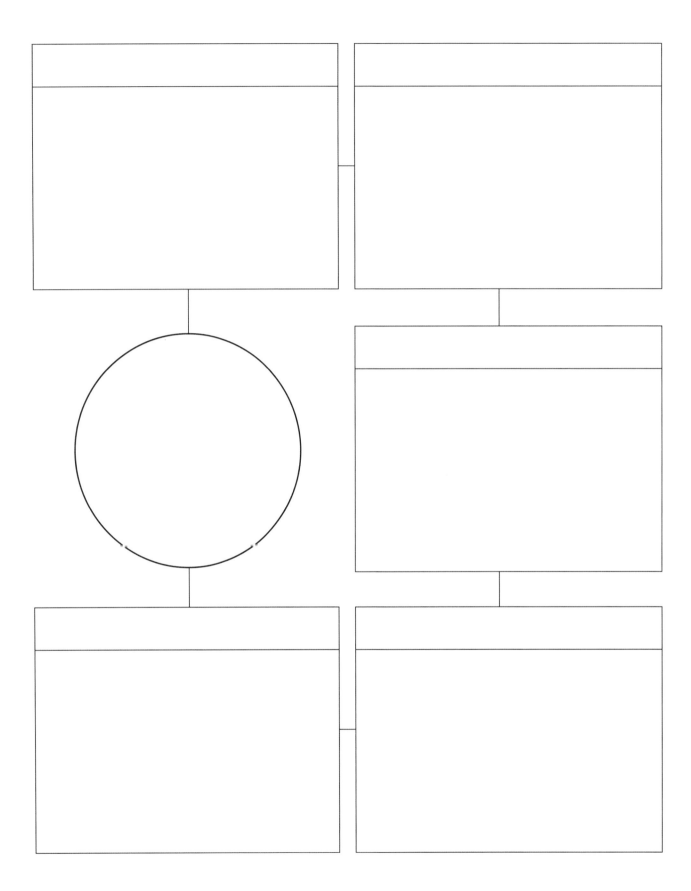

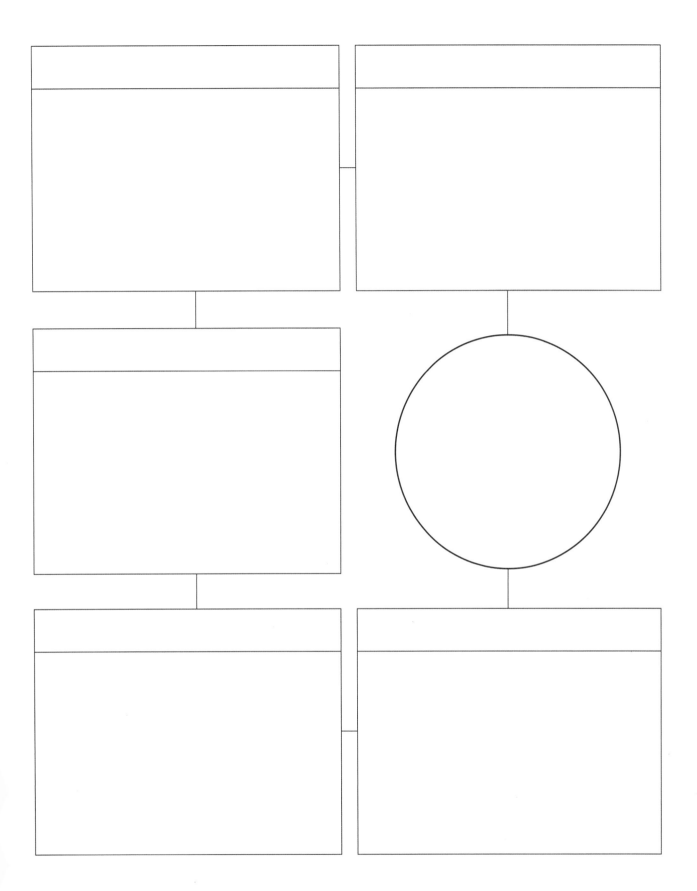

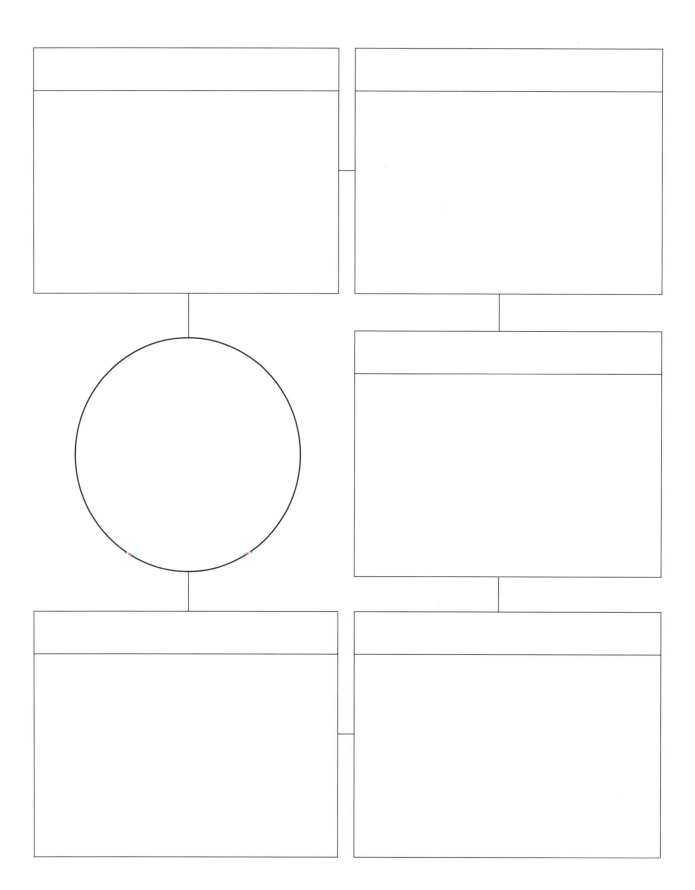

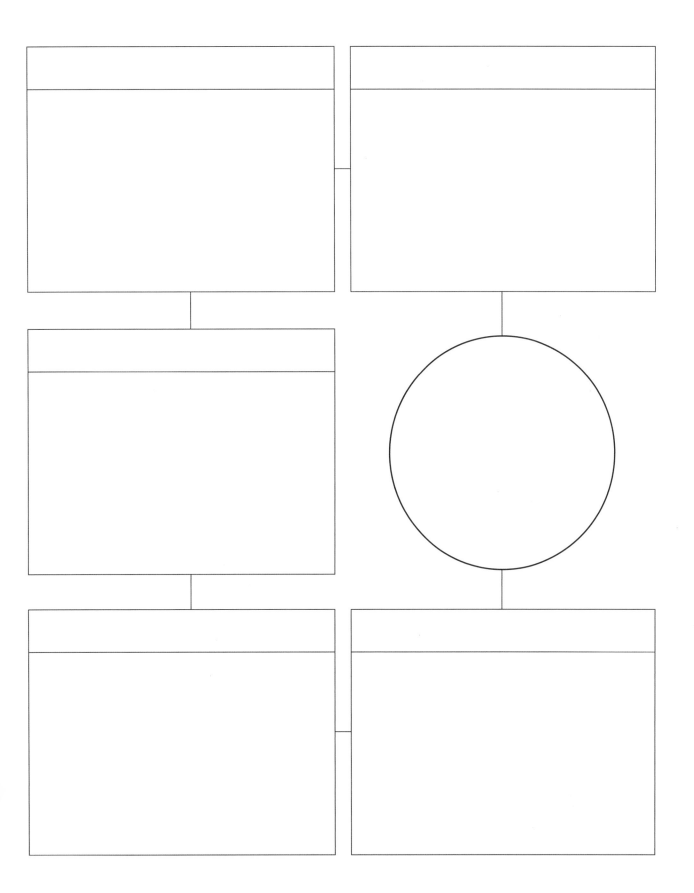

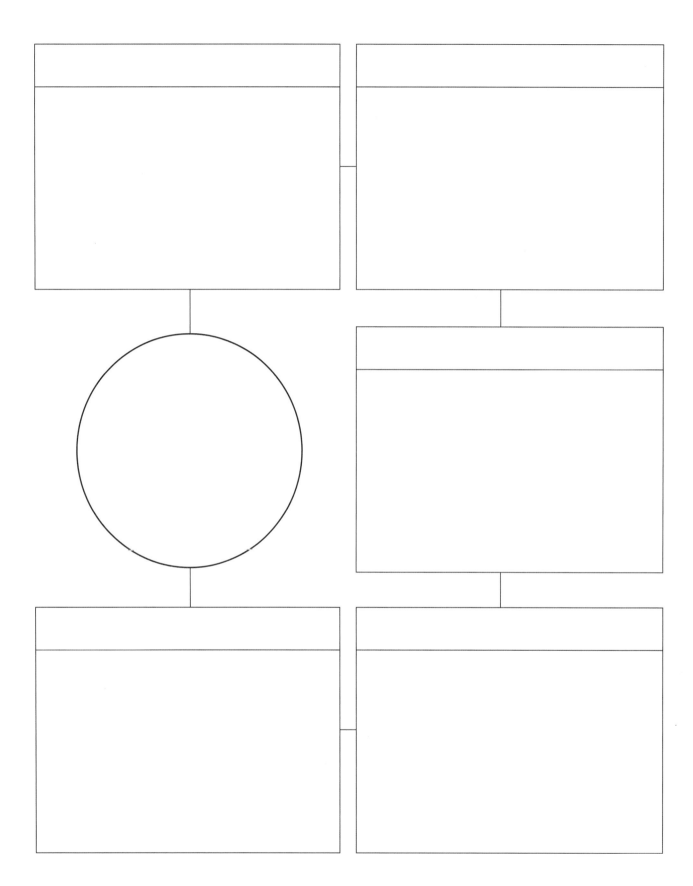

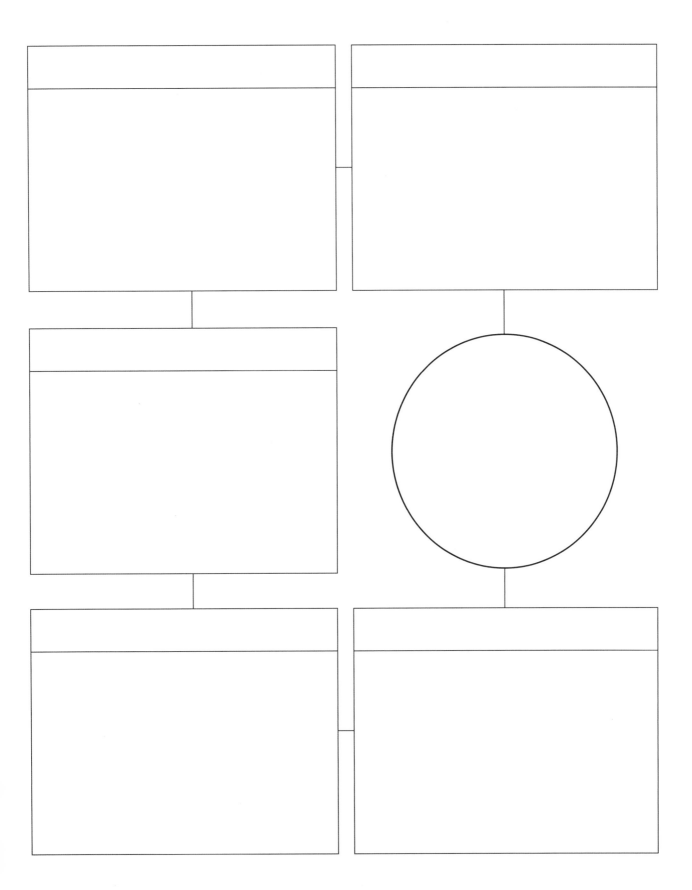

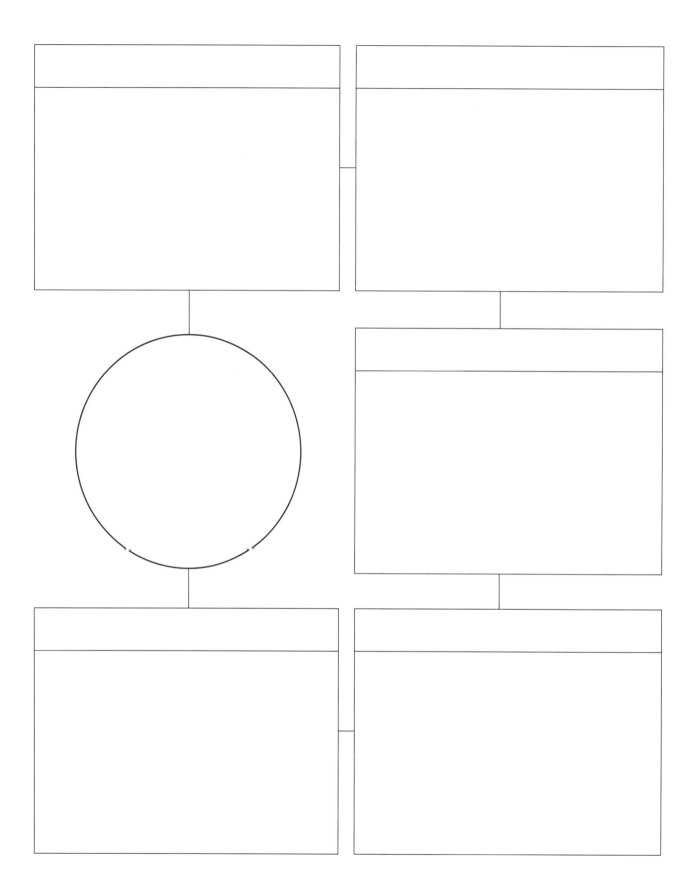

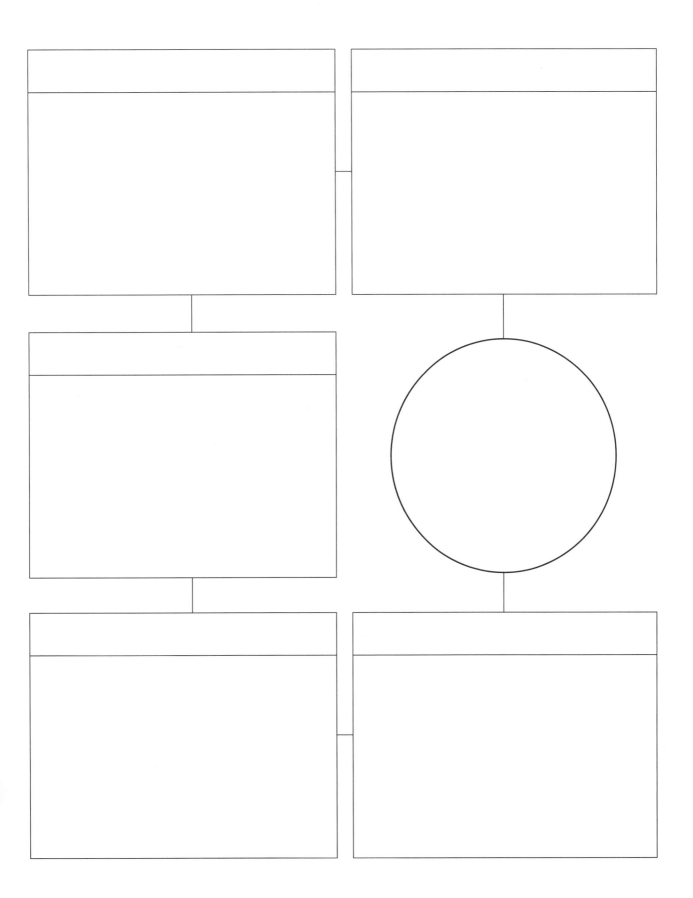

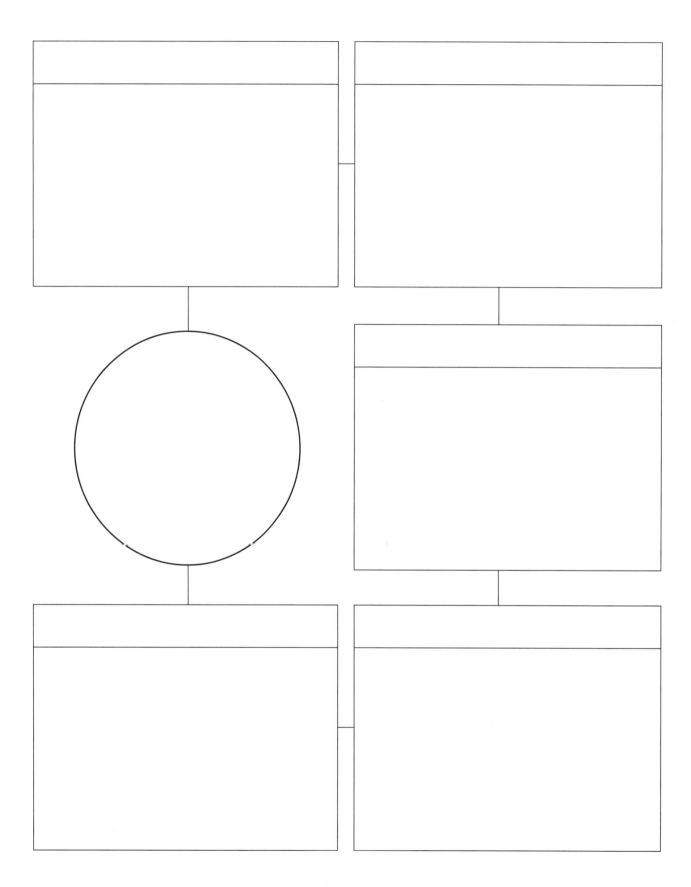

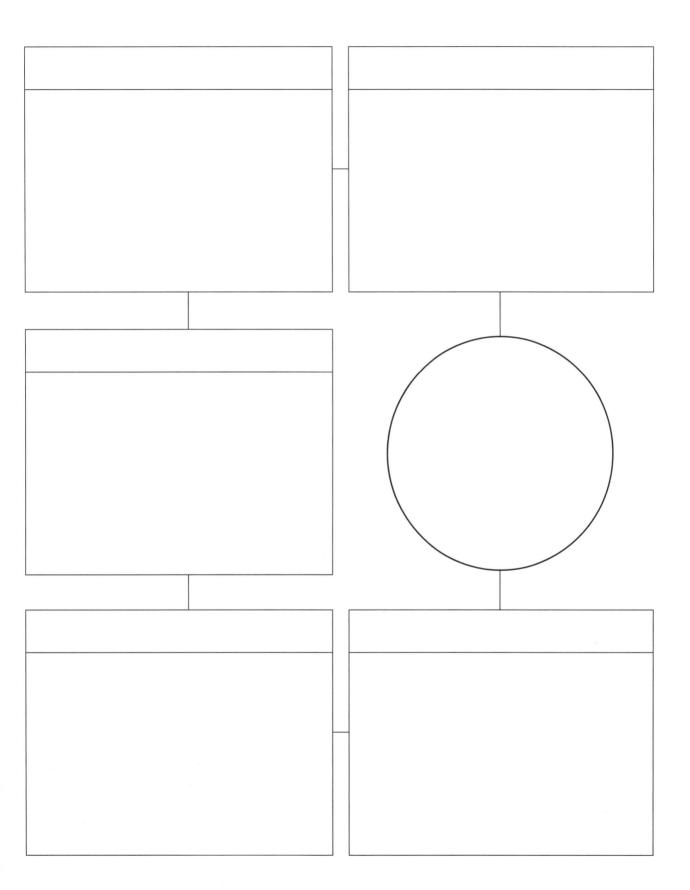

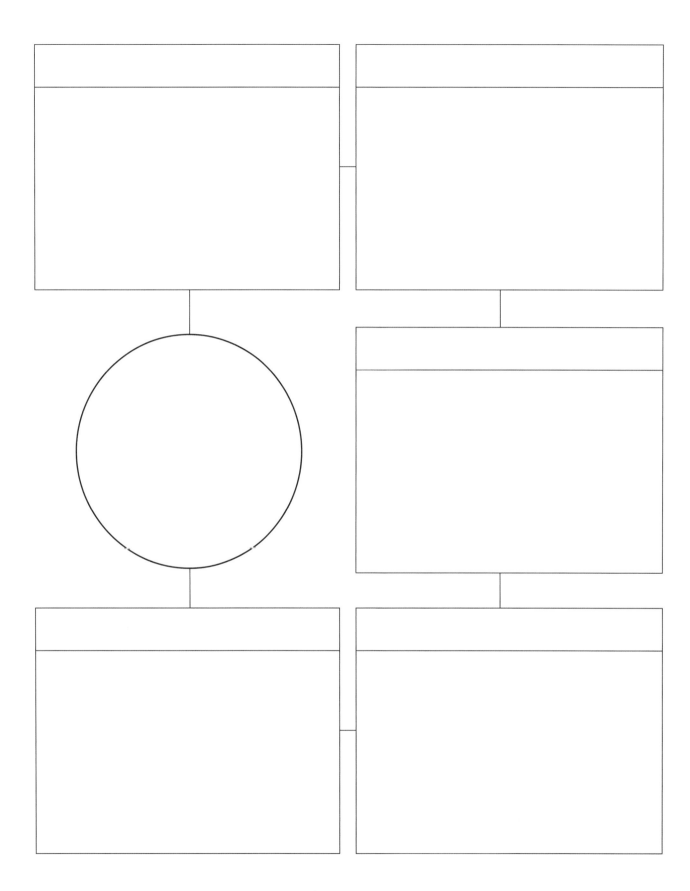

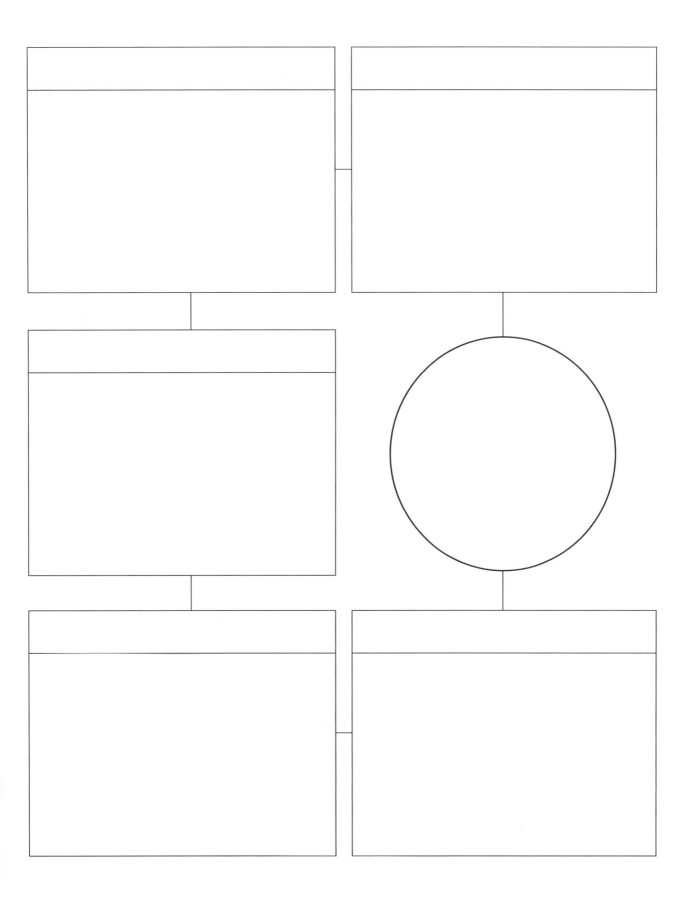

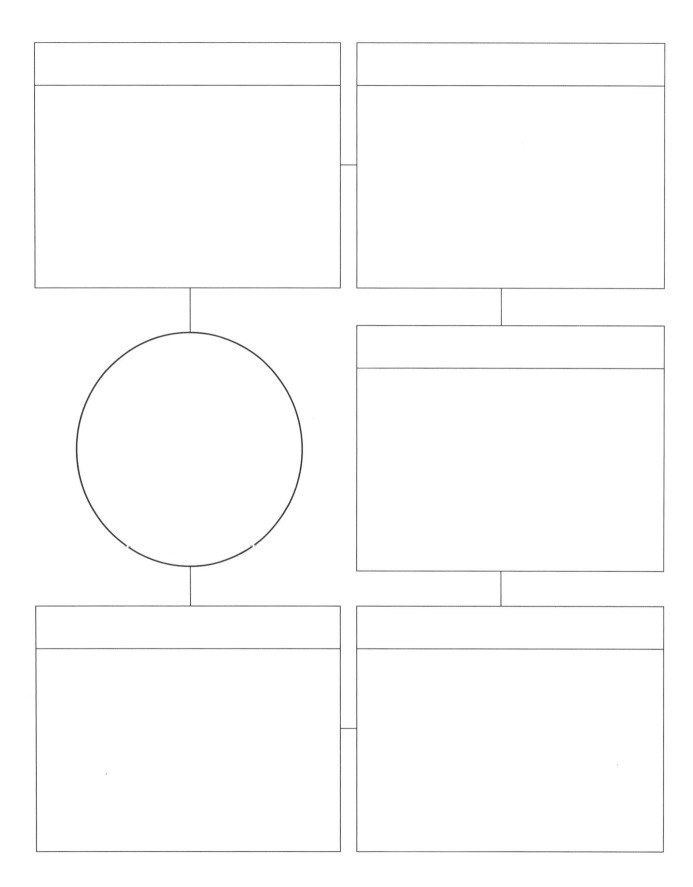

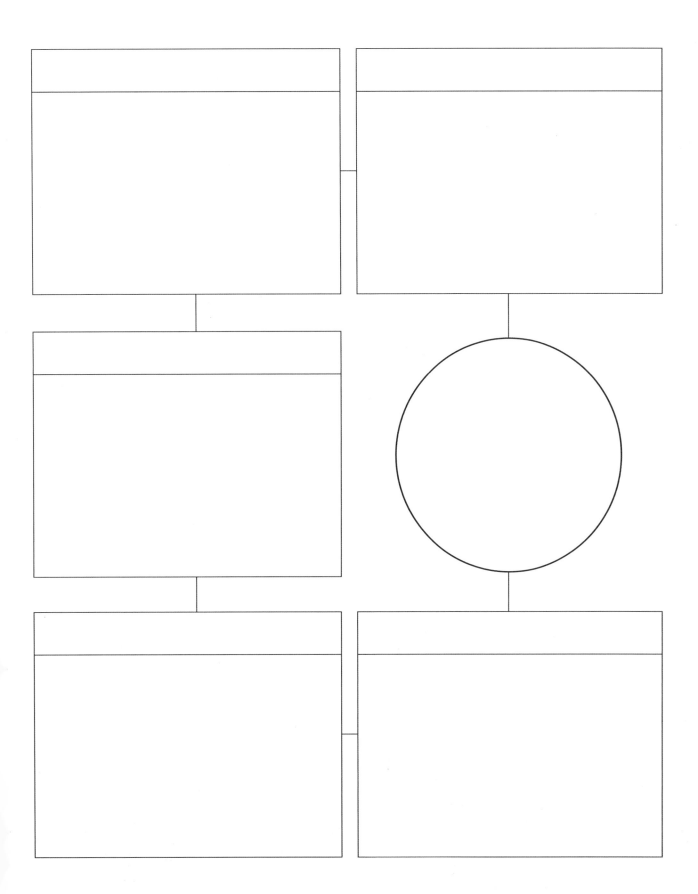

THE ART OF FERMENTATION:
BRIDGING TRADITION AND INNOVATION

Fermentation, a transformative and time-honored culinary technique, has long been a cornerstone of traditional recipes across the American continent. This ancient biological process, perfected by ancestral cultures, not only preserved food and enhanced its nutritional value but also infused dishes and beverages with distinctive flavors and textures. Today, the legacy of fermentation continues to evolve, blending seamlessly with contemporary practices to create a rich, dynamic culinary heritage.

GLOBAL FUSION: EXPANDING THE FERMENTATION PALETTE

Incorporating fermentation practices from Asian, Middle Eastern, and European cuisines can further enrich your culinary repertoire. Imagine blending the tangy complexity of Korean kimchi with the earthy flavors of traditional Mesoamerican corn. Or infuse your dishes with the umami depth of Japanese miso, the vibrant spice of Middle Eastern preserved lemons, or the savory richness of European sauerkraut. These cross-cultural combinations not only enhance the flavor profiles of your creations but also highlight the universal appeal of fermentation as a technique that transcends borders. By fusing these divorce traditions, you can create a truly global palette of fermented foods that reflects the innovative spirit of contemporary cooking.

Fermenting foods is both an art and a science, capable of transforming simple ingredients into probiotic-rich, flavorful delights. To master this craft, consider these five essential factors when embarking on your fermentation journey:

- **SANITATION:** Ensure all utensils, containers, and your working area are thoroughly cleaned and sanitized to prevent unwanted bacteria or mold from contaminating your ferment.

- **TEMPERATURE:** Most fermentation processes require specific temperature ranges to encourage the right bacteria to grow while inhibiting harmful ones. Typically, this is around 55°F to 75°F (13°C to 24°C).

- **SALT CONCENTRATION:** Salt is critical in fermentation for flavor and safety. It inhibits the growth of undesirable bacteria while promoting the growth of beneficial lactobacilli. The correct amount of salt is crucial; too little may lead to spoilage, while too much can hinder fermentation.

- **TIME:** Fermentation is not a rushed process. The required time can vary significantly depending on the type of food, the size of the pieces, the salt concentration, and the fermentation temperature. Monitor the process and taste periodically to decide when it has reached the desired flavor and texture.

- **OXYGEN EXPOSURE:** Many types of fermentation require anaerobic conditions (the absence of oxygen) to prevent the growth of mold and yeast on the surface. Methods to reduce exposure to air include using airlocks, weights to submerge food, and proper container sealing.

TRADITIONAL FERMENTATION PRACTICES

Historically, fermentation has been integral to the culinary identity of Central and South American cultures. Beverages like chicha, made from maize, cassava, or other grains, and pulque, derived from the fermented sap of the agave plant, are emblematic of the region's rich heritage. These drinks, often associated with ceremonial and daily consumption, embody the spiritual and communal aspects of ancient societies. In cuisine, using fermented corn in tamales and arepas demonstrates how fermentation is essential in making grains more digestible and nutritious.

CONTEMPORARY FERMENTATION PRACTICES

In contemporary kitchens, the principles of fermentation continue to thrive, enriched by both innovation and a resurgence of interest in traditional methods. Modern chefs and home cooks are exploring the depths of flavor fermentation can bring to food and beverages. For example, the revival of artisanal pulque production reflects a renewed appreciation for ancestral beverages, while the popularity of kombucha showcases the global influence on local fermentation practices.

Contemporary cuisine also sees the fermentation of vegetables and legumes, inspired by global traditions such as kimchi and sauerkraut, being adapted to include local ingredients like jalapeños, carrots, and black beans. This not only enhances the dishes' flavor profiles but also boosts their probiotic content, aligning with modern dietary trends focused on gut health.

FUSION AND INNOVATION

Fusing traditional and contemporary fermentation practices has given rise to innovative culinary creations. Fermented salsas and mojos featuring local fruits, chilies, and herbs offer complex flavors that complement various dishes, from grilled meats to vegan bowls. Chefs are experimenting with fermented nut cheeses, blending the ancient art of fermentation with modern veganism to produce sustainable, flavorful alternatives to dairy.

SUSTAINABILITY AND REVIVAL

Embracing fermentation reflects a broader movement towards sustainability and the revival of ancient wisdom in the kitchen. By fermenting locally sourced ingredients, contemporary practices pay homage to the ancestral understanding of the land and its yields. This approach not only minimizes waste and extends the shelf life of produce but also strengthens the connection between modern communities and their culinary heritage.

CONCLUSION

The ongoing dialogue between ancestral and contemporary cultures through fermentation underscores a deep respect for tradition while embracing innovation possibilities. This culinary alchemy, evolving within the kitchens of Central and South America, continues to enrich the global culinary landscape, offering profound insights into the past and promising pathways for the future.

SUGGESTED APPLICATIONS

In these recipes, we want to showcase the innovative spirit of contemporary Central and South American cuisines, respecting ancestral techniques while exploring new culinary frontiers. Through fermentation, we not only preserve but also enhance our meals with complex flavors, improved digestibility, and increased nutritional value, celebrating the enduring legacy of Mesoamerican cultures. These suggestions offer a glimpse into the potential of incorporating fermentation processes into your kitchen.

FERMENTED SUNFLOWER SEED SPREAD

- **INGREDIENTS:** Sunflower seeds, garlic, salt, water.

- **PROCESS:** Soak sunflower seeds, blend with garlic and salt, and add enough water to achieve a creamy consistency. Ferment for 1–2 days at room temperature. A versatile spread that adds a nutty, tangy flavor to sandwiches and crackers.

FERMENTED PUMPKIN SEED PESTO

- **INGREDIENTS:** Pumpkin seeds, basil, garlic, lemon juice, olive oil, salt.

- **PROCESS:** Combine all ingredients in a food processor, then ferment the pesto daily to enhance its flavors. Perfect for pasta, sandwiches, and as a dip.

CHIA SEED KOMBUCHA

- **INGREDIENTS:** Brewed kombucha, chia seeds.

- **PROCESS:** Add chia seeds to the finished kombucha and let sit for 24 hours until the seeds have expanded and suspended, creating a nutrient-dense, probiotic-rich beverage.

NOTES

_____

_____

_____

_____

_____

_____

NUTS

WALNUT KVASS

- **INGREDIENTS:** Walnuts, water, sugar, bread, yeast.

- **PROCESS:** Boil walnuts, strain and add sugar to the water, cool to room temperature, add bread yeast, and ferment for 5-7 days. Walnut Kvass is a traditional fermented drink with a unique taste and health benefits.

COCONUT KEFIR

- **INGREDIENTS:** Coconut water, kefir grains.

- **PROCESS:** Add kefir grains to coconut water and let ferment at room temperature for 24-48 hours until it becomes slightly fizzy and tangy. Coconut kefir is a delicious, dairy-free probiotic drink.

MACADAMIA NUT SOUR CREAM

- **INGREDIENTS:** Macadamia nuts, water, lemon juice, probiotic capsule.

- **PROCESS:** Blend soaked macadamia nuts with water, lemon juice, and the contents of a probiotic capsule. Let ferment overnight for a tangy, creamy, vegan sour cream.

NOTES

_____

_____

_____

_____

_____

_____

FERMENTED OAT AND BERRY BREAKFAST BOWL

- **INGREDIENTS:** Rolled oats, mixed berries, kefir or yogurt, honey.

- **PROCESS:** Mix oats with kefir or yogurt, add a layer of berries, drizzle with honey, and let ferment overnight. Serve as a nutritious and digestible breakfast option.

SORGHUM BEER

- **INGREDIENTS:** Sorghum malt, hops, yeast, water.

- **PROCESS:** Brew sorghum malt with hops, cool the mixture, add yeast, and ferment for about a week. Sorghum beer is a gluten-free alternative to traditional barley beer, rich in flavor.

MACADAMIA NUT SOUR CREAM

- **INGREDIENTS:** Sprouted amaranth, water.

- **PROCESS:** Blend sprouted amaranth with water, strain, and let the liquid ferment at room temperature for 2-3 days to create a probiotic drink that aids digestion.

NOTES

_____

_____

_____

_____

_____

_____

LEGUMES

FERMENTED LENTIL DIP

- **INGREDIENTS:** Cooked lentils, tahini, garlic, lemon juice, salt.

- **PROCESS:** Blend all ingredients until smooth, then allow to ferment at room temperature for 1-2 days. This dip combines the nutritional benefits of lentils with the probiotic effects of fermentation.

BLACK BEAN SOY SAUCE SUBSTITUTE

- **INGREDIENTS:** Black beans, salt, water.

- **PROCESS:** Mash cooked black beans with salt, cover with water, and let ferment for 1-2 weeks—strain to obtain a fermented black bean sauce that is soy-free and umami-rich.

PEA MISO

- **INGREDIENTS:** Green peas, koji (rice inoculated with Aspergillus oryzae), salt.

- **PROCESS:** Mash cooked green peas, mix with koji and salt, pack into a jar, and ferment for 6 months to a year. Green pea miso is a unique, sweet alternative to traditional soy miso, adding depth to dishes.

NOTES

_____

_____

_____

_____

_____

_____

ALMOND REJUVELAC

- **INGREDIENTS:** Raw almonds, water.

- **PROCESS:** Soak almonds, blend with water, strain, and ferment the liquid at room temperature for 2-3 days. Almond rejuvelac can be used as a probiotic drink or as a starter culture for other fermentations.

CASHEW YOGURT

- **INGREDIENTS:** Cashews, water, probiotic capsules.

- **PROCESS:** Blend soaked cashews with water until smooth, stir in probiotic powder, and let ferment overnight in a warm place. This creamy yogurt enriches breakfast bowls and smoothies with its tang and nutritional benefits.

PISTACHIO CHEESE

- **INGREDIENTS:** Pistachios, water, probiotic capsules, salt.

- **PROCESS:** Blend soaked pistachios with water and probiotic powder, then ferment for 24-48 hours—season with salt, shape, and age in the refrigerator for a firmer texture.

NOTES

_____

_____

_____

_____

_____

_____

FERMENTED GRAIN & LEGUME

QUINOA SOURDOUGH STARTER

- **INGREDIENTS:** Quinoa flour, water.
- **PROCESS:** Mix quinoa flour with water and let it sit warmly. Feed it daily with equal parts flour and water. Use this gluten-free starter to make bread and pancakes.

CHICKPEA TEMPEH

- **INGREDIENTS:** Chickpeas, tempeh starter (Rhizopus oligosporus).
- **PROCESS:** Cook chickpeas, dehull, mix with tempeh starter, and ferment for 24-48 hours at a warm temperature. Slice and fry this tempeh for a hearty addition to meals.

LENTIL BEER

- **INGREDIENTS:** Lentils, malted barley, hops, yeast.
- **PROCESS:** Mash cooked lentils with malted barley, boil with hops, cool, add yeast, and ferment for 7-14 days. This innovative beer combines traditional brewing with lentils' nutritional powerhouse.

NOTES

_____
_____
_____
_____
_____
_____

FERMENTED HOT SAUCES

Spiciness has been an integral part of Mesoamerican cuisine for thousands of years, deeply rooted in the culinary traditions of ancient cultures like the Maya and Aztecs. These civilizations revered chili peppers not only for their flavor but also for their medicinal and spiritual properties. Spiciness was used to balance dishes, add complexity, and preserve foods in the warm climates of Central and South America. Chili peppers were often combined with other native ingredients like cacao, tomatoes, and corn to create rich, flavorful sauces that became the cornerstone of their gastronomy.

Today, the legacy of using spiciness to enhance flavors continues through the art of crafting hot sauces. These sauces do more than just add heat—they can introduce unexpected flavor profiles that complement and elevate your dishes. By incorporating elements like fruits, herbs, and spices, hot sauces inspired by ancient traditions can transform a meal, adding depth and complexity that surprise and delight the palate. Whether drizzled over grilled vegetables, stirred into stews, or used as a marinade, these sauces pay homage to the rich culinary heritage of Mesoamerican cultures while enhancing modern-day culinary creations.

SWEET & SPICY

RECIPE	DESCRIPTION	FUSION
MANGO HABANERO WITH GINGER	A tropical blend of ripe mangoes and fiery habanero peppers infused with fresh ginger for a sweet and spicy kick with warmth from the ginger.	Mesoamerican peppers with Asian ginger.
PINEAPPLE ANCHO CHILI WITH TURMERIC	Sweet pineapple pairs with the smoky, mild heat of ancho chilies, enhanced with earthy turmeric for a complex, sweet, and spicy sauce.	Mesoamerican peppers with Asian turmeric.
FIG CHIPOTLE WITH BALSAMIC VINEGAR	Dried figs bring sweetness, balanced by the smoky heat of chipotle peppers and the rich acidity of balsamic vinegar for a unique sweet and spicy flavor.	Mesoamerican peppers with European balsamic vinegar.

RECIPE	DESCRIPTION	FUSION
SERRANO PEPPER WITH MISO	Fresh serrano peppers fermented with umami-rich miso paste create a salty and spicy hot sauce with deep, savory undertones.	Mesoamerican peppers with Japanese miso.
PINEAPPLE ANCHO CHILI WITH TURMERIC	Jalapeños combine with salty olive brine and the herbal, nutty flavors of za'atar to create a vibrant, salty, and spicy sauce.	Mesoamerican peppers with Middle Eastern za'atar.
GUAJILLO CHILI WITH SOY SAUCE AND GARLIC	The mild heat and smoky flavor of guajillo chilies are enhanced with salty soy sauce and fermented garlic for a rich, salty, and spicy condiment.	Mesoamerican peppers with Asian soy sauce.

CITRUS & SPICY

RECIPE	DESCRIPTION	FUSION
LIME AND THAI BIRD CHILI	Tangy lime juice meets the intense heat of Thai bird chilies, fermented together for a bright, citrusy hot sauce with a powerful spicy finish.	Mesoamerican peppers with Asian Thai bird chili.
ORANGE HABANERO WITH CUMIN AND CORIANDER	Sweet orange juice and zest paired with the fiery heat of habanero peppers, rounded out by earthy cumin and coriander seeds for a citrusy, spicy sauce.	Mesoamerican peppers with Middle Eastern spices.
YUZU AND PASILLA CHILI	The mild, fruity heat of pasilla chilies is complemented by the tart and fragrant yuzu citrus, resulting in a complex citrus and spicy hot sauce.	Mesoamerican peppers with Japanese yuzu.

HERBAL & SPICY

RECIPE	DESCRIPTION	FUSION
BASIL JALAPEÑO WITH LEMON	Fresh jalapeños fermented with aromatic basil and tangy lemon juice creating a vibrant, herbal, and spicy sauce with a refreshing citrus note.	Mesoamerican peppers with Mediterranean basil.
LEMON VERBENA AND FRESNO CHILI	Lemon verbena's fragrant citrus notes paired with the bright heat of Fresno chilies, resulting in a delicate yet spicy sauce with a subtle herbal finish.	Mesoamerican peppers with Mediterranean lemon verbena.
LEMONGRASS AND POBLANO PEPPER	Mild poblano peppers combined with the citrusy and slightly sweet flavor of lemongrass create a balanced hot sauce with a fresh, herbal-spicy taste.	Mesoamerican peppers with Asian lemongrass.

ENHANCING FLAVORS & TEXTURES:
ELABORATING FILLINGS & TOPPINGS

These plant-based powerhouses, revered by ancient civilizations, offer more than just sustenance; they are deeply embedded in the cultural and spiritual practices of the Maya, Aztecs, and other indigenous peoples. In this companion book, we invite you to rediscover the profound culinary potential of grains, nuts, seeds, and legumes within the Mesoamerican tradition and to explore how they can seamlessly replace animal-based proteins in a way that honors both the past and the future of our shared table.

In this exploration of Mesoamerican cuisine, it is essential to recognize the remarkable potential of these ingredients as not only traditional staples but also as modern substitutes for animal-based proteins. The inherent nutritional richness of grains, nuts, seeds, and legumes—packed with essential amino acids, vitamins, and minerals—mirrors the ingenuity of our ancestors who crafted vibrant, flavorful dishes from these humble yet powerful foods.

These ingredients provide diverse textures and flavors that can elevate any dish, allowing us to experience the true essence of Mesoamerican cuisine in a way that is both authentic and innovative. Whether it's the nutty richness of amaranth, the earthy depth of beans, or the crisp freshness of toasted pumpkin seeds, each ingredient tells a story of resilience, creativity, and nourishment that continues to inspire modern plant-based cooking.

ENHANCING FLAVORS & TEXTURES: ELABORATING FILLINGS & TOPPINGS

LEGUMES

The Protein Powerhouse; Legumes like lentils, chickpeas, and beans are excellent plant-based protein sources. They are versatile enough for various dishes, from hearty stews and soups to burgers and spreads. Lentils can replace ground meat in dishes like shepherd's pie or tacos, while chickpeas can be transformed into falafel or creamy hummus.

A Flavorful Foundation; Legumes like lentils, chickpeas, and beans are naturally earthy and hearty, making them excellent flavor carriers. They readily absorb the spices, herbs, and sauces they're cooked with. For instance, slow-cooking lentils in a rich tomato and spice base can produce a flavorful dish reminiscent of traditional meat stews. Chickpeas can be roasted with spices to create a crispy, savory snack or blended into a rich, garlicky hummus that bursts with flavor.

NUTS

A Crunchy, Protein-Rich Substitute; Nuts such as almonds, walnuts, and cashews are not only rich in protein but also packed with healthy fats. They can be used to create plant-based versions of creamy sauces, such as cashew cream or almond ricotta, which serve as excellent alternatives to dairy-based options. Ground nuts can also be added to veggie burgers or used as a crust for plant-based protein dishes.

Richness and Depth; Nuts such as almonds, walnuts, and cashews bring a rich, buttery flavor to dishes. They can be toasted to enhance their nuttiness or blended into smooth butter and creams that add a luxurious texture and depth of flavor to sauces, soups, and desserts. Cashew cream, for example, can replace dairy cream in savory dishes, adding a subtly sweet and nutty flavor that complements a wide range of spices and vegetables.

SEEDS

Small but Mighty: Seeds like chia, flax, and hemp are nutrient-dense and protein-rich. For a protein boost, add them to smoothies, oatmeal, or yogurt. Flaxseeds, when ground and mixed with water, create a gel-like consistency that can replace eggs in baking, making them a valuable ingredient for plant-based cooking.

A Punch of Flavor; Seeds like chia, flax, sesame, and hemp pack a flavorful punch despite their small size. Toasted sesame seeds, for example, can add a nutty, slightly sweet flavor to salads, stir-fries, and baked goods. Flaxseeds bring a mild, earthy taste and can be used in baking as an egg substitute, contributing to both the flavor and texture of the dish. Hemp seeds, with their slightly nutty flavor, can be sprinkled over salads or blended into smoothies to add a subtle richness.

GRAINS

A Foundation for Plant-Based Protein; While grains like quinoa, farro, and millet are often considered carbohydrates, they also provide a good amount of protein. Quinoa, in particular, is a complete protein containing all nine essential amino acids. It can be used as a base for salads, bowls, or stuffed vegetables, offering a satisfying and protein-rich alternative to meat.

Versatile Flavor Bases; Grains such as quinoa, farro, and barley offer a neutral canvas that can be infused with various flavors. Quinoa's mild nuttiness pairs well with both sweet and savory ingredients, making it a versatile base for salads, pilafs, and even breakfast bowls. Cooking grains in vegetable broth or with aromatic herbs and spices can elevate their flavor, transforming them from simple side dishes into the star of the meal.

CREATIVE CULINARY APPLICATIONS

Incorporating these plant-based proteins into your diet doesn't mean sacrificing flavor or texture. Consider using blended nuts and seeds to create rich pâtés or spreads, or experiment with legumes in unexpected ways, such as in desserts or plant-based meat substitutes. Grains can be used to make hearty pilafs or stuffed into vegetables for a protein-packed meal. Combining different grains, nuts, seeds, and legumes can create a complete protein profile. For example, pairing beans with rice or nuts with seeds can ensure you get all the essential amino acids your body needs.

One of the most exciting aspects of using grains, nuts, seeds, and legumes is the opportunity to experiment with

flavor pairings. Combining these ingredients with fresh herbs, citrus, spices, and umami-rich elements like miso or nutritional yeast can create layers of complex flavors. For example, a grain bowl with quinoa, roasted vegetables, and a tahini-lemon dressing offers a balance of nuttiness, brightness, and earthiness that is both satisfying and vibrant.

Umami, the savory taste often associated with meat, can also be achieved with plant-based ingredients. Fermented foods like miso, soy sauce, and nutritional yeast add a deep, savory flavor that enhances the natural richness of nuts, seeds, and legumes. Roasting or caramelizing these ingredients can also bring out their natural umami qualities, creating dishes that are full of depth and complexity.

Dare to be extraordinaire, do not be afraid to think outside the box regarding flavor. Use spices and herbs generously, explore global flavor profiles, and experiment with cooking techniques like roasting, fermenting, and toasting to bring out the best in your plant-based proteins. For instance, adding smoky paprika or chipotle to black beans can mimic the depth of flavor found in traditional meat dishes, while a touch of citrus zest can brighten up a nut-based sauce.

IN THE HEART OF MESOAMERICAN CULINARY TRADITION: EXPANDING PLANT-BASED POSSIBILITIES

As we explore the vibrant culinary landscape of

Mesoamerica, we are reminded of the deep connection between the land and its people. Grains, nuts, seeds, and legumes have long been at the core of Mesoamerican diets, offering a rich source of nutrition and flavor. Yet, the innovative spirit of these ancient cultures extends even further, inspiring us to incorporate a wider array of plant-based ingredients into our modern interpretations of traditional dishes.

In addition to the time-honored staples of grains, nuts, seeds, and legumes, the diverse and fertile lands of Mesoamerica provide us with other remarkable plant-based alternatives to animal proteins. Mushrooms, with their meaty texture and earthy flavor, have been a beloved ingredient in Mesoamerican cuisine for centuries. They are perfect for adding depth and umami to dishes, often standing in for meat in stews, tacos, and tamales.

Jackfruit, another plant-based powerhouse, has gained recognition for its ability to mimic the texture of pulled pork or shredded chicken. This tropical fruit, native to regions close to Mesoamerica, seamlessly integrates into traditional recipes, bringing a subtle sweetness that enhances savory dishes. Hearts of palm, for example, offer a tender, delicate texture that can be used instead of seafood in ceviches and salads. At the same time, cactus paddles (nopales) add a unique, slightly tangy flavor and a satisfying crunch to various dishes.

By incorporating these diverse plant-based ingredients into our culinary repertoire, we continue the legacy of Mesoamerican innovation, honoring the land's bounty while embracing modern dietary trends. These ingredients not only provide essential nutrients but also allow us to create dishes that are rich in flavor, texture, and tradition. Let this journey inspire you to connect with the wisdom of the past while crafting meals that nourish both body and soul in the present.

FILLINGS

Fillings are the heart of many culinary creations, transforming simple dishes into rich, flavorful experiences. In this section, we explore a variety of plant-based fillings that draw inspiration from Mesoamerican traditions while embracing global influences. These fillings are designed to add depth, texture, and vibrant flavors to your recipes, making them ideal for everything from tacos and empanadas to tamales and stuffed vegetables. Whether you're looking for something savory, spicy, or sweet, these fillings offer endless possibilities to elevate your plant-based cooking, bringing both innovation and tradition to your table.

FILLING	DESCRIPTION	BEST USED FOR
MUSHROOM AND NOPAL CACTUS TAMALE FILLING	Sautéed mushrooms, diced nopales (cactus paddles), and traditional Mesoamerican spices wrapped in masa and steamed in corn husks.	Tamales
JACKFRUIT AND BLACK BEAN BARBACOA	Shredded jackfruit and black beans, slow-cooked with smoky chipotle, cumin, and Mexican oregano.	Tacos, burritos, enchiladas
QUINOA AND AMARANTH STUFFED PEPPERS	Sweet bell peppers stuffed with quinoa, amaranth, and finely chopped vegetables, seasoned with ancho chili powder and lime.	Stuffed peppers
CHICKPEA AND SWEET POTATO EMPANADA FILLING	Roasted sweet potatoes and chickpeas, spiced with cinnamon and allspice, inspired by Yucatán flavors, wrapped in a flaky pastry.	Empanadas

FILLING	DESCRIPTION	BEST USED FOR
PUMPKIN SEED (PEPITA) AND ROASTED POBLANO FILLING	Ground pumpkin seeds blended with roasted poblanos, garlic, and cilantro for a creamy, nutty filling.	Enchiladas, tamales
SPICY BLACK BEAN AND SWEET CORN	Black beans, sweet corn, sautéed onions, chipotle peppers, cumin, and cinnamon.	Burritos, enchiladas, quesadillas
BUTTERNUT SQUASH AND MOLE POBLANO	Roasted butternut squash in rich mole poblano sauce with chocolate and chili.	Tamales, stuffed chiles
PINTO BEAN AND QUINOA CHILI FILLING	Pinto beans, quinoa, tomatoes, garlic, and chili spices.	Burritos, empanadas, stuffed peppers

FILLING	DESCRIPTION	BEST USED FOR
ROASTED POBLANO AND POTATO RAJAS	Roasted potatoes, charred poblano strips, sautéed onions, garlic, and oregano.	Tacos, sopes, tamales
SMOKY TEMPEH AND PLANTAIN FILLING	Crumbled tempeh in adobo sauce with sautéed plantains, offering a smoky, sweet flavor.	Tacos, burritos, empanadas
CHIPOTLE-LIME MARINATED TOFU AND AVOCADO	Grilled chipotle-lime marinated tofu with avocado slices.	Tacos, wraps, lettuce cups
RED QUINOA AND CHAYOTE SQUASH	Nutty red quinoa with sautéed chayote squash, seasoned with epazote and lime.	Enchiladas stuffed tomatoes

FILLING	DESCRIPTION	BEST USED FOR
CILANTRO-LIME RICE AND BLACK-EYED PEA FILLING	Fluffy cilantro-lime rice mixed with tender black-eyed peas.	Burritos, tacos, bowls
SMOKY EGGPLANT AND TOMATO SOFRITO	Roasted eggplant with a tomato-based sofrito of onions, garlic, and smoked paprika.	Empanadas, quesadillas, stuffed zucchini
GREEN LENTIL AND TOMATILLO FILLING	Green lentils cooked with tangy tomatillos, garlic, and cumin.	Tacos, tamales, stuffed chiles

TOPPINGS

Toppings are the finishing touch that can elevate a dish from ordinary to extraordinary. In this section, we explore a variety of dry and liquid plant-based toppings that add layers of flavor, texture, and visual appeal to your meals. From crunchy crumbles and nutty blends to creamy drizzles and tangy glazes, these toppings are designed to enhance your culinary creations, making every bite more dynamic and delicious. Whether you're looking to add a burst of umami, a hint of spice, or a touch of sweetness, these versatile toppings offer endless possibilities to transform your dishes into something exceptional.

TOPPING	DESCRIPTION	BEST USED FOR
SPICED PEPITA (PUMPKIN SEED) CRUMBLE	A crunchy topping made from roasted and spiced pumpkin seeds blended with smoked paprika, garlic powder, and sea salt.	Soups, salads, roasted vegetables, avocado toast
CRISPY CHICKPEA CRUMBLE	Roasted chickpeas seasoned with cumin, coriander, and chili powder, crushed into a coarse crumble.	Grain bowls, salads, pasta dishes
NUTRITIONAL YEAST AND HERB BLEND	A dry topping made from nutritional yeast mixed with dried herbs like oregano, thyme, and parsley for a cheesy, umami flavor.	Popcorn, pasta, roasted vegetables, casseroles

TOPPING	DESCRIPTION	BEST USED FOR
TOASTED SESAME AND FLAX SEED MIX	A nutrient-rich blend of toasted sesame and flax seeds, lightly seasoned with sea salt and lemon zest.	Stir-fries, salads, smoothies, baked goods
CHILI-LIME CASHEW CRUMBLE	Roasted cashews tossed with chili powder, lime zest, and maple syrup, crushed into a coarse crumble.	Tacos, nachos, grain bowls, soups
AVOCADO-LIME CREMA	A smooth and creamy topping made from blended avocado, lime juice, and garlic, offering a refreshing and tangy flavor.	Tacos, burritos, enchiladas, grilled vegetables
SMOKY CHIPOTLE CASHEW SAUCE	A rich, smoky sauce made from soaked cashews and chipotle peppers in adobo, garlic, and lime.	Roasted vegetables, grilled tofu, tacos, grain bowls

TOPPING	DESCRIPTION	BEST USED FOR
TAHINI-GARLIC DRIZZLE	A nutty and savory sauce made from tahini, garlic, lemon juice, and salt, thinned to a smooth drizzle.	Roasted root vegetables, falafel, salads, grain bowls
MISO-GINGER DRESSING	A tangy and umami-rich dressing made from white miso paste, fresh ginger, rice vinegar, and sesame oil.	Salads, steamed vegetables, grain bowls, marinades
POMEGRANATE MOLASSES GLAZE	A sweet and tangy glaze made from pomegranate molasses, olive oil, and balsamic vinegar, offering a rich, fruity flavor.	Roasted Brussels sprouts, grilled eggplant, Mediterranean dishes
MUSHROOM AND SUNFLOWER SEED DUKKAH	A savory topping made from toasted sunflower seeds, dried mushrooms, cumin, coriander, and sesame seeds.	Roasted vegetables, salads, hummus, crust for tofu or tempeh

TOPPING	DESCRIPTION	BEST USED FOR
SHIITAKE MUSHROOM AND SESAME SEED CRUMBLE	Dried shiitake mushrooms ground into a powder mixed with toasted sesame seeds, nutritional yeast, and sea salt.	Ramen, stir-fries, roasted vegetables, popcorn
MUSHROOM AND PUMPKIN SEED SALSA	A chunky salsa made from sautéed mushrooms, roasted pumpkin seeds, garlic, and lime juice.	Tacos, grilled vegetables, grain bowls, salads
TRUFFLE-INFUSED MUSHROOM OIL	A luxurious oil infused with dried mushrooms and truffle essence, capturing deep, earthy flavors with a hint of truffle.	Pasta, risotto, roasted vegetables, soups, flatbreads
CHANTERELLE MUSHROOM AND HEMP SEED PESTO	A twist on traditional pesto, made with sautéed chanterelle mushrooms, basil, garlic, hemp seeds, and olive oil.	Sandwiches, pasta, roasted vegetables, dip for crusty bread

RECIPES AND NOTES

RECIPE

PREP TIME	DATE	CATEGORY
COOKING TIME	SERVINGS	PAIRING
TOTAL TIME	FUSION	PAGE REFERENCE

INGREDIENTS	PROCEDURE

NOTES

RECIPE

PREP TIME	DATE	CATEGORY
COOKING TIME	SERVINGS	PAIRING
TOTAL TIME	FUSION	PAGE REFERENCE

INGREDIENTS	PROCEDURE

NOTES

RECIPE

PREP TIME	DATE	CATEGORY
COOKING TIME	SERVINGS	PAIRING
TOTAL TIME	FUSION	PAGE REFERENCE

INGREDIENTS	PROCEDURE

NOTES

RECIPE

PREP TIME	DATE	CATEGORY
COOKING TIME	SERVINGS	PAIRING
TOTAL TIME	FUSION	PAGE REFERENCE

INGREDIENTS	PROCEDURE

NOTES

RECIPE

PREP TIME	DATE	CATEGORY
COOKING TIME	SERVINGS	PAIRING
TOTAL TIME	FUSION	PAGE REFERENCE

INGREDIENTS	PROCEDURE

NOTES

RECIPE

PREP TIME	DATE	CATEGORY
COOKING TIME	SERVINGS	PAIRING
TOTAL TIME	FUSION	PAGE REFERENCE

INGREDIENTS	PROCEDURE

NOTES

RECIPE

PREP TIME	DATE	CATEGORY
COOKING TIME	SERVINGS	PAIRING
TOTAL TIME	FUSION	PAGE REFERENCE

INGREDIENTS	PROCEDURE

NOTES

RECIPE

PREP TIME	DATE	CATEGORY
COOKING TIME	SERVINGS	PAIRING
TOTAL TIME	FUSION	PAGE REFERENCE

INGREDIENTS	PROCEDURE

NOTES

RECIPE

PREP TIME	DATE	CATEGORY
COOKING TIME	SERVINGS	PAIRING
TOTAL TIME	FUSION	PAGE REFERENCE

INGREDIENTS	PROCEDURE

NOTES

RECIPE

PREP TIME	DATE	CATEGORY
COOKING TIME	SERVINGS	PAIRING
TOTAL TIME	FUSION	PAGE REFERENCE

INGREDIENTS	PROCEDURE

NOTES

RECIPE

PREP TIME	DATE	CATEGORY
COOKING TIME	SERVINGS	PAIRING
TOTAL TIME	FUSION	PAGE REFERENCE

INGREDIENTS	PROCEDURE

NOTES

RECIPE

PREP TIME	DATE	CATEGORY
COOKING TIME	SERVINGS	PAIRING
TOTAL TIME	FUSION	PAGE REFERENCE

INGREDIENTS	PROCEDURE

NOTES

RECIPE

PREP TIME	DATE	CATEGORY
COOKING TIME	SERVINGS	PAIRING
TOTAL TIME	FUSION	PAGE REFERENCE

INGREDIENTS	PROCEDURE

NOTES

RECIPE

PREP TIME	DATE	CATEGORY
COOKING TIME	SERVINGS	PAIRING
TOTAL TIME	FUSION	PAGE REFERENCE

INGREDIENTS	PROCEDURE

NOTES

RECIPE

PREP TIME	DATE	CATEGORY
COOKING TIME	SERVINGS	PAIRING
TOTAL TIME	FUSION	PAGE REFERENCE

INGREDIENTS	PROCEDURE

NOTES

RECIPE

PREP TIME	DATE	CATEGORY
COOKING TIME	SERVINGS	PAIRING
TOTAL TIME	FUSION	PAGE REFERENCE

INGREDIENTS	PROCEDURE

NOTES

RECIPE

PREP TIME	DATE	CATEGORY
COOKING TIME	SERVINGS	PAIRING
TOTAL TIME	FUSION	PAGE REFERENCE

INGREDIENTS	PROCEDURE

NOTES

RECIPE

PREP TIME	DATE	CATEGORY
COOKING TIME	SERVINGS	PAIRING
TOTAL TIME	FUSION	PAGE REFERENCE

INGREDIENTS	PROCEDURE

NOTES

RECIPE

PREP TIME	DATE	CATEGORY
COOKING TIME	SERVINGS	PAIRING
TOTAL TIME	FUSION	PAGE REFERENCE

INGREDIENTS	PROCEDURE

NOTES

RECIPE

PREP TIME	DATE	CATEGORY
COOKING TIME	SERVINGS	PAIRING
TOTAL TIME	FUSION	PAGE REFERENCE

INGREDIENTS	PROCEDURE

NOTES

RECIPE

PREP TIME	DATE	CATEGORY
COOKING TIME	SERVINGS	PAIRING
TOTAL TIME	FUSION	PAGE REFERENCE

INGREDIENTS	PROCEDURE

NOTES

RECIPE

PREP TIME	DATE	CATEGORY
COOKING TIME	SERVINGS	PAIRING
TOTAL TIME	FUSION	PAGE REFERENCE

INGREDIENTS	PROCEDURE

NOTES

RECIPE

PREP TIME	DATE	CATEGORY
COOKING TIME	SERVINGS	PAIRING
TOTAL TIME	FUSION	PAGE REFERENCE

INGREDIENTS	PROCEDURE

NOTES

RECIPE

PREP TIME	DATE	CATEGORY
COOKING TIME	SERVINGS	PAIRING
TOTAL TIME	FUSION	PAGE REFERENCE

INGREDIENTS	PROCEDURE

NOTES

RECIPE

PREP TIME	DATE	CATEGORY
COOKING TIME	SERVINGS	PAIRING
TOTAL TIME	FUSION	PAGE REFERENCE

INGREDIENTS	PROCEDURE

NOTES

RECIPE

PREP TIME	DATE	CATEGORY
COOKING TIME	SERVINGS	PAIRING
TOTAL TIME	FUSION	PAGE REFERENCE

INGREDIENTS	PROCEDURE

NOTES

RECIPE

PREP TIME	DATE	CATEGORY
COOKING TIME	SERVINGS	PAIRING
TOTAL TIME	FUSION	PAGE REFERENCE

INGREDIENTS	PROCEDURE

NOTES

RECIPE

PREP TIME	DATE	CATEGORY
COOKING TIME	SERVINGS	PAIRING
TOTAL TIME	FUSION	PAGE REFERENCE

INGREDIENTS	PROCEDURE

NOTES

RECIPE

PREP TIME	DATE	CATEGORY
COOKING TIME	SERVINGS	PAIRING
TOTAL TIME	FUSION	PAGE REFERENCE

INGREDIENTS	PROCEDURE

NOTES

RECIPE

PREP TIME	DATE	CATEGORY
COOKING TIME	SERVINGS	PAIRING
TOTAL TIME	FUSION	PAGE REFERENCE

INGREDIENTS	PROCEDURE

NOTES

RECIPE

PREP TIME	DATE	CATEGORY
COOKING TIME	SERVINGS	PAIRING
TOTAL TIME	FUSION	PAGE REFERENCE

INGREDIENTS	PROCEDURE

NOTES

RECIPE

PREP TIME	DATE	CATEGORY
COOKING TIME	SERVINGS	PAIRING
TOTAL TIME	FUSION	PAGE REFERENCE

INGREDIENTS	PROCEDURE

NOTES

RECIPE

PREP TIME	DATE	CATEGORY
COOKING TIME	SERVINGS	PAIRING
TOTAL TIME	FUSION	PAGE REFERENCE

INGREDIENTS	PROCEDURE

NOTES

RECIPE

PREP TIME	DATE	CATEGORY
COOKING TIME	SERVINGS	PAIRING
TOTAL TIME	FUSION	PAGE REFERENCE

INGREDIENTS	PROCEDURE

NOTES

RECIPE

PREP TIME	DATE	CATEGORY
COOKING TIME	SERVINGS	PAIRING
TOTAL TIME	FUSION	PAGE REFERENCE

INGREDIENTS	PROCEDURE

NOTES

RECIPE

PREP TIME	DATE	CATEGORY
COOKING TIME	SERVINGS	PAIRING
TOTAL TIME	FUSION	PAGE REFERENCE

INGREDIENTS	PROCEDURE

NOTES

RECIPE

PREP TIME	DATE	CATEGORY
COOKING TIME	SERVINGS	PAIRING
TOTAL TIME	FUSION	PAGE REFERENCE

INGREDIENTS	PROCEDURE

NOTES

RECIPE

PREP TIME	DATE	CATEGORY
COOKING TIME	SERVINGS	PAIRING
TOTAL TIME	FUSION	PAGE REFERENCE

INGREDIENTS	PROCEDURE

NOTES

RECIPE

PREP TIME	DATE	CATEGORY
COOKING TIME	SERVINGS	PAIRING
TOTAL TIME	FUSION	PAGE REFERENCE

INGREDIENTS	PROCEDURE

NOTES

RECIPE

PREP TIME	DATE	CATEGORY
COOKING TIME	SERVINGS	PAIRING
TOTAL TIME	FUSION	PAGE REFERENCE

INGREDIENTS	PROCEDURE

NOTES

RECIPE

PREP TIME	DATE	CATEGORY
COOKING TIME	SERVINGS	PAIRING
TOTAL TIME	FUSION	PAGE REFERENCE

INGREDIENTS	PROCEDURE

NOTES

RECIPE

PREP TIME	DATE	CATEGORY
COOKING TIME	SERVINGS	PAIRING
TOTAL TIME	FUSION	PAGE REFERENCE

INGREDIENTS	PROCEDURE

NOTES

RECIPE

PREP TIME	DATE	CATEGORY
COOKING TIME	SERVINGS	PAIRING
TOTAL TIME	FUSION	PAGE REFERENCE

INGREDIENTS	PROCEDURE

NOTES

RECIPE

PREP TIME	DATE	CATEGORY
COOKING TIME	SERVINGS	PAIRING
TOTAL TIME	FUSION	PAGE REFERENCE

INGREDIENTS	PROCEDURE

NOTES

RECIPE

PREP TIME	DATE	CATEGORY
COOKING TIME	SERVINGS	PAIRING
TOTAL TIME	FUSION	PAGE REFERENCE

INGREDIENTS	PROCEDURE

NOTES

RECIPE

PREP TIME	DATE	CATEGORY
COOKING TIME	SERVINGS	PAIRING
TOTAL TIME	FUSION	PAGE REFERENCE

INGREDIENTS	PROCEDURE

NOTES

RECIPE

PREP TIME	DATE	CATEGORY
COOKING TIME	SERVINGS	PAIRING
TOTAL TIME	FUSION	PAGE REFERENCE

INGREDIENTS	PROCEDURE

NOTES

RECIPE

PREP TIME	DATE	CATEGORY
COOKING TIME	SERVINGS	PAIRING
TOTAL TIME	FUSION	PAGE REFERENCE

INGREDIENTS	PROCEDURE

NOTES

RECIPE

PREP TIME	DATE	CATEGORY
COOKING TIME	SERVINGS	PAIRING
TOTAL TIME	FUSION	PAGE REFERENCE

INGREDIENTS	PROCEDURE

NOTES

RECIPE

PREP TIME	DATE	CATEGORY
COOKING TIME	SERVINGS	PAIRING
TOTAL TIME	FUSION	PAGE REFERENCE

INGREDIENTS	PROCEDURE

NOTES

RECIPE

PREP TIME	DATE	CATEGORY
COOKING TIME	SERVINGS	PAIRING
TOTAL TIME	FUSION	PAGE REFERENCE

INGREDIENTS	PROCEDURE

NOTES

RECIPE

PREP TIME	DATE	CATEGORY
COOKING TIME	SERVINGS	PAIRING
TOTAL TIME	FUSION	PAGE REFERENCE

INGREDIENTS	PROCEDURE

NOTES

RECIPE

PREP TIME	**DATE**	**CATEGORY**
COOKING TIME	**SERVINGS**	**PAIRING**
TOTAL TIME	**FUSION**	**PAGE REFERENCE**

INGREDIENTS

PROCEDURE

NOTES

RECIPE

PREP TIME	DATE	CATEGORY
COOKING TIME	SERVINGS	PAIRING
TOTAL TIME	FUSION	PAGE REFERENCE

INGREDIENTS	PROCEDURE

NOTES

RECIPE

PREP TIME	DATE	CATEGORY
COOKING TIME	SERVINGS	PAIRING
TOTAL TIME	FUSION	PAGE REFERENCE

INGREDIENTS	PROCEDURE

NOTES

RECIPE

PREP TIME	DATE	CATEGORY
COOKING TIME	SERVINGS	PAIRING
TOTAL TIME	FUSION	PAGE REFERENCE

INGREDIENTS	PROCEDURE

NOTES

RECIPE

PREP TIME	DATE	CATEGORY
COOKING TIME	SERVINGS	PAIRING
TOTAL TIME	FUSION	PAGE REFERENCE

INGREDIENTS	PROCEDURE

NOTES

RECIPE

PREP TIME	DATE	CATEGORY
COOKING TIME	SERVINGS	PAIRING
TOTAL TIME	FUSION	PAGE REFERENCE

INGREDIENTS	PROCEDURE

NOTES

RECIPE

PREP TIME	DATE	CATEGORY
COOKING TIME	SERVINGS	PAIRING
TOTAL TIME	FUSION	PAGE REFERENCE

INGREDIENTS	PROCEDURE

NOTES

RECIPE

PREP TIME	DATE	CATEGORY
COOKING TIME	SERVINGS	PAIRING
TOTAL TIME	FUSION	PAGE REFERENCE

INGREDIENTS	PROCEDURE

NOTES

RECIPE

PREP TIME	DATE	CATEGORY
COOKING TIME	SERVINGS	PAIRING
TOTAL TIME	FUSION	PAGE REFERENCE

INGREDIENTS	PROCEDURE

NOTES

RECIPE

PREP TIME	DATE	CATEGORY
COOKING TIME	SERVINGS	PAIRING
TOTAL TIME	FUSION	PAGE REFERENCE

INGREDIENTS	PROCEDURE

NOTES

RECIPE

PREP TIME	DATE	CATEGORY
COOKING TIME	SERVINGS	PAIRING
TOTAL TIME	FUSION	PAGE REFERENCE

INGREDIENTS	PROCEDURE

NOTES

RECIPE

PREP TIME	DATE	CATEGORY
COOKING TIME	SERVINGS	PAIRING
TOTAL TIME	FUSION	PAGE REFERENCE

INGREDIENTS	PROCEDURE

NOTES

RECIPE

PREP TIME	DATE	CATEGORY
COOKING TIME	SERVINGS	PAIRING
TOTAL TIME	FUSION	PAGE REFERENCE

INGREDIENTS	PROCEDURE

NOTES

RECIPE

PREP TIME	DATE	CATEGORY
COOKING TIME	SERVINGS	PAIRING
TOTAL TIME	FUSION	PAGE REFERENCE

INGREDIENTS	PROCEDURE

NOTES

RECIPE

PREP TIME	DATE	CATEGORY
COOKING TIME	SERVINGS	PAIRING
TOTAL TIME	FUSION	PAGE REFERENCE

INGREDIENTS	PROCEDURE

NOTES

RECIPE

PREP TIME	DATE	CATEGORY
COOKING TIME	SERVINGS	PAIRING
TOTAL TIME	FUSION	PAGE REFERENCE

INGREDIENTS	PROCEDURE

NOTES

RECIPE

PREP TIME	DATE	CATEGORY
COOKING TIME	SERVINGS	PAIRING
TOTAL TIME	FUSION	PAGE REFERENCE

INGREDIENTS	PROCEDURE

NOTES

RECIPE

PREP TIME	DATE	CATEGORY
COOKING TIME	SERVINGS	PAIRING
TOTAL TIME	FUSION	PAGE REFERENCE

INGREDIENTS	PROCEDURE

NOTES

RECIPE

PREP TIME	DATE	CATEGORY
COOKING TIME	SERVINGS	PAIRING
TOTAL TIME	FUSION	PAGE REFERENCE

INGREDIENTS	PROCEDURE

NOTES

RECIPE

PREP TIME	DATE	CATEGORY
COOKING TIME	SERVINGS	PAIRING
TOTAL TIME	FUSION	PAGE REFERENCE

INGREDIENTS	PROCEDURE

NOTES

RECIPE

PREP TIME	DATE	CATEGORY
COOKING TIME	SERVINGS	PAIRING
TOTAL TIME	FUSION	PAGE REFERENCE

INGREDIENTS	PROCEDURE

NOTES

RECIPE

PREP TIME	DATE	CATEGORY
COOKING TIME	SERVINGS	PAIRING
TOTAL TIME	FUSION	PAGE REFERENCE

INGREDIENTS	PROCEDURE

NOTES

RECIPE

PREP TIME	DATE	CATEGORY
COOKING TIME	SERVINGS	PAIRING
TOTAL TIME	FUSION	PAGE REFERENCE

INGREDIENTS	PROCEDURE

NOTES

RECIPE

PREP TIME	DATE	CATEGORY
COOKING TIME	SERVINGS	PAIRING
TOTAL TIME	FUSION	PAGE REFERENCE

INGREDIENTS	PROCEDURE

NOTES

RECIPE

PREP TIME	DATE	CATEGORY
COOKING TIME	SERVINGS	PAIRING
TOTAL TIME	FUSION	PAGE REFERENCE

INGREDIENTS	PROCEDURE

NOTES

RECIPE

PREP TIME	DATE	CATEGORY
COOKING TIME	SERVINGS	PAIRING
TOTAL TIME	FUSION	PAGE REFERENCE

INGREDIENTS	PROCEDURE

NOTES

RECIPE

PREP TIME	DATE	CATEGORY
COOKING TIME	SERVINGS	PAIRING
TOTAL TIME	FUSION	PAGE REFERENCE

INGREDIENTS	PROCEDURE

NOTES

RECIPE

PREP TIME	DATE	CATEGORY
COOKING TIME	SERVINGS	PAIRING
TOTAL TIME	FUSION	PAGE REFERENCE

INGREDIENTS	PROCEDURE

NOTES

RECIPE

PREP TIME	DATE	CATEGORY
COOKING TIME	SERVINGS	PAIRING
TOTAL TIME	FUSION	PAGE REFERENCE

INGREDIENTS	PROCEDURE

NOTES

RECIPE

PREP TIME	DATE	CATEGORY
COOKING TIME	SERVINGS	PAIRING
TOTAL TIME	FUSION	PAGE REFERENCE

INGREDIENTS	PROCEDURE

NOTES

RECIPE

PREP TIME	DATE	CATEGORY
COOKING TIME	SERVINGS	PAIRING
TOTAL TIME	FUSION	PAGE REFERENCE

INGREDIENTS	PROCEDURE

NOTES

RECIPE

PREP TIME	DATE	CATEGORY
COOKING TIME	SERVINGS	PAIRING
TOTAL TIME	FUSION	PAGE REFERENCE

INGREDIENTS	PROCEDURE

NOTES

RECIPE

PREP TIME	DATE	CATEGORY
COOKING TIME	SERVINGS	PAIRING
TOTAL TIME	FUSION	PAGE REFERENCE

INGREDIENTS	PROCEDURE

NOTES

RECIPE

PREP TIME	DATE	CATEGORY
COOKING TIME	SERVINGS	PAIRING
TOTAL TIME	FUSION	PAGE REFERENCE

INGREDIENTS	PROCEDURE

NOTES

RECIPE

PREP TIME	DATE	CATEGORY
COOKING TIME	SERVINGS	PAIRING
TOTAL TIME	FUSION	PAGE REFERENCE

INGREDIENTS	PROCEDURE

NOTES

RECIPE

PREP TIME	DATE	CATEGORY
COOKING TIME	SERVINGS	PAIRING
TOTAL TIME	FUSION	PAGE REFERENCE

INGREDIENTS	PROCEDURE

NOTES

RECIPE

PREP TIME	DATE	CATEGORY
COOKING TIME	SERVINGS	PAIRING
TOTAL TIME	FUSION	PAGE REFERENCE

INGREDIENTS	PROCEDURE

NOTES

RECIPE

PREP TIME	DATE	CATEGORY
COOKING TIME	SERVINGS	PAIRING
TOTAL TIME	FUSION	PAGE REFERENCE

INGREDIENTS	PROCEDURE

NOTES

RECIPE

PREP TIME	DATE	CATEGORY
COOKING TIME	SERVINGS	PAIRING
TOTAL TIME	FUSION	PAGE REFERENCE

INGREDIENTS	PROCEDURE

NOTES

RECIPE

PREP TIME	DATE	CATEGORY
COOKING TIME	SERVINGS	PAIRING
TOTAL TIME	FUSION	PAGE REFERENCE

INGREDIENTS	PROCEDURE

NOTES

FROM FIELDS TO FEAST;
A PLANT-BASED EXTRAVAGANZA

Drawing inspiration from the rich traditions of Mesoamerican cuisine, this collection brings together bold flavors, vibrant colors, and satisfying textures, transforming your plant-based feast into a true celebration of the land's bounty. Let this epic meal serve as a testament to the power of plant-based cooking and the enduring legacy of Mesoamerican culinary heritage, which continues to influence kitchens worldwide.

By blending the essence of Mesoamerican flavors with the diverse culinary traditions of Asia and the Mediterranean, we've curated a selection of recipes that will captivate your guests, sparking excitement and anticipation for a meal they won't soon forget. We have made a set of categories for you to assemble a menu of your liking, including drinks, tacos, chilaquiles, escabeches, ceviches, salsas, empanadas, skillets, barbacoas, casseroles, and, of course, desserts!

CHILAQUILES

PUMPKIN SEED AND TOMATILLO CHILAQUILES:

Tortilla chips tossed in a tangy tomatillo and roasted pumpkin seed sauce, garnished with fresh avocado slices, pickled red onions, and a sprinkle of plant-based queso fresco.

RED MOLE CHILAQUILES:

Corn tortillas soaked in a rich red mole sauce, topped with sautéed mushrooms, plant-based crema, and a scattering of toasted sesame seeds.

MEDITERRANEAN CHILAQUILES WITH ROASTED RED PEPPER AND OLIVE TAPENADE:

Tortilla chips tossed in a roasted red pepper sauce infused with kalamata olives, garlic, and capers, topped with a Mediterranean-inspired plant-based feta, fresh basil, and a drizzle of balsamic reduction.

ASIAN-STYLE CHILAQUILES WITH MISO-TAMARI SAUCE:

Tortilla chips are tossed in a savory miso-tamari sauce with shiitake mushrooms and scallions. The dish is topped with toasted sesame seeds and fresh cilantro and served with a side of pickled ginger.

CEVICHES

MANGO AND JICAMA CEVICHE:

Diced mango, jicama, and cucumber tossed with lime juice, chili, and fresh cilantro, served with crispy plantain chips.

HEARTS OF PALM AND AVOCADO CEVICHE:

Hearts of palm and creamy avocado mixed with tomatoes, red onions, and a zesty lime marinade, served on tostadas.

MEDITERRANEAN CHICKPEA AND ARTICHOKE CEVICHE:

A refreshing mix of chickpeas, marinated artichoke hearts, tomatoes, red onion, and cucumber tossed in a lemon-oregano dressing and served with grilled pita bread.

ASIAN-INSPIRED MANGO AND COCONUT CEVICHE:

Mango, coconut meat, and cucumber marinated in a lime-ginger dressing with fresh mint and Thai basil, topped with a sprinkle of chili flakes, and served with crispy wonton chips.

TACOS

CHIPOTLE JACKFRUIT TACOS: Shredded jackfruit simmered in a smoky chipotle sauce, topped with fresh cilantro, pickled jalapeños, and a squeeze of lime.

MUSHROOM AND NOPAL TACOS: Grilled mushrooms and nopal (cactus) paddles sprinkled with cotija-style vegan cheese and a drizzle of avocado-lime crema.

MEDITERRANEAN FALAFEL TACOS WITH TZATZIKI: Crispy falafel balls wrapped in soft tortillas, cucumber-tomato salad, vegan tzatziki, and a sprinkle of fresh dill.

ASIAN TERIYAKI TOFU TACOS: Marinated tofu grilled and drizzled with teriyaki sauce, topped with crunchy Asian slaw made of shredded cabbage, carrots, and sesame seeds, served with a drizzle of sriracha mayo.

EMPANADAS

SWEET POTATO AND BLACK BEAN EMPANADAS:

Flaky pastry filled with roasted sweet potatoes, black beans, and a touch of cinnamon and allspice, baked to golden perfection.

MEDITERRANEAN SPINACH AND PINE NUT EMPANADAS:

Flaky pastry filled with sautéed spinach, pine nuts, and sun-dried tomatoes, seasoned with garlic and lemon zest, served with a side of marinara sauce for dipping.

ASIAN SWEET POTATO AND EDAMAME EMPANADAS:

A sweet and savory filling of mashed sweet potatoes and edamame, seasoned with soy sauce, ginger, and a hint of miso, wrapped in golden pastry, served with a sesame-soy dipping sauce.

PLANTAIN AND REFRIED BEAN EMPANADAS:

A sweet and savory filling of ripe plantains and refried beans encased in a crispy dough, these empanadas are served with a side of salsa verde.

ESCABECHES

PICKLED CARROT AND CAULIFLOWER ESCABECHE: A vibrant mix of carrots, cauliflower, and jalapeños pickled in a tangy vinegar brine with oregano and garlic, perfect as a side or a topping for tacos.

MEDITERRANEAN EGGPLANT AND ZUCCHINI ESCABECHE: Marinated eggplant and zucchini with garlic, rosemary, and white wine vinegar; this dish is served as a tangy and aromatic side dish or topping for flatbreads.

ASIAN-INSPIRED RADISH AND DAIKON ESCABECHE: Crisp radishes and daikon pickled in rice vinegar, ginger, and sesame oil brine, perfect as a tangy side or topping for rice bowls and noodles.

GREEN BEAN AND TOMATILLO ESCABECHE: Green beans and tomatillos are pickled with onions, garlic, and bay leaves, offering a tangy, slightly spicy accompaniment to any dish.

SALSAS

MEDITERRANEAN OLIVE AND SUN-DRIED TOMATO SALSA:

A chunky salsa made with chopped kalamata olives, sun-dried tomatoes, capers, and fresh parsley, with a splash of red wine vinegar, perfect for topping bruschetta or pita chips.

ASIAN-INSPIRED PINEAPPLE AND GINGER SALSA:

This sweet and spicy salsa, which combines diced pineapple, fresh ginger, red chili, and cilantro with a dash of soy sauce and lime juice, is ideal for pairing with grilled vegetables or tofu.

ROASTED TOMATILLO AND AVOCADO SALSA:

A creamy blend of roasted tomatillos, avocado, and cilantro, with a hint of garlic and lime, ideal for dipping or topping tacos.

SPICY CHIPOTLE AND PINEAPPLE SALSA:

This smoky and sweet salsa combines chipotle peppers and diced pineapple. It's perfect for pairing with grilled vegetables or as a taco topping.

SKILLETS

MEXICAN STREET CORN SKILLET:

Sweet corn sautéed with vegan butter, chili powder, and lime, topped with fresh cilantro, vegan mayo, and crumbled plant-based cheese.

SWEET POTATO AND POBLANO SKILLET:

Roasted sweet potatoes and poblanos sautéed with onions and garlic, finished with a drizzle of spiced tahini sauce.

MEDITERRANEAN RATATOUILLE SKILLET:

A colorful medley of eggplant, zucchini, bell peppers, and tomatoes, sautéed with garlic and herbes de Provence, finished with a drizzle of olive oil and fresh basil, served with crusty bread.

ASIAN-INSPIRED STIR-FRY SKILLET WITH TOFU AND BOK CHOY:

This savory stir-fry features tofu, bok choy, shiitake mushrooms, and snap peas cooked in a ginger-soy sauce and finished with sesame oil and toasted sesame seeds.

BARBACOA

MUSHROOM AND LENTIL BARBACOA:

This rich and hearty barbacoa is made with mushrooms and lentils, slow-cooked in a smoky adobo sauce. It's perfect for stuffing tacos or serving over rice.

JACKFRUIT AND BLACK BEAN BARBACOA:

A plant-based take on traditional barbacoa using shredded jackfruit and black beans simmered with chipotle, cumin, and Mexican oregano.

MEDITERRANEAN MUSHROOM AND LENTIL BARBACOA:

A rich and hearty barbacoa with portobello mushrooms and lentils, slow-cooked with garlic, rosemary, and red wine, and served with couscous or flatbread.

ASIAN BBQ JACKFRUIT BARBACOA:

Jackfruit cooked in a sweet and tangy hoisin-based BBQ sauce, served with steamed buns or over jasmine rice, garnished with fresh scallions and sesame seeds.

CASSEROLES

MEDITERRANEAN EGGPLANT AND RICOTTA LASAGNA:
Layers of roasted eggplant, vegan ricotta, tomates verdes, and salsa de tomate are topped with plant-based mozzarella and baked until bubbly. It is served with a side of garlic bread.

ASIAN-INSPIRED MISO AND VEGETABLE LASAGNA:
A fusion lasagna with layers of miso-infused béchamel sauce, sautéed mushrooms, bok choy, and tofu, topped with panko breadcrumbs and baked until golden, served with a side of pickled vegetables.

BUTTERNUT SQUASH AND SPINACH CASSEROLE:
Layers of roasted butternut squash, sautéed spinach, and cashew ricotta are topped with a rich tomato sauce and baked until bubbly.

POBLANO AND BLACK BEAN LASAGNA:
A spicy and flavorful lasagna featuring roasted poblanos, black beans, and a creamy plant-based cheese sauce layered with corn tortillas instead of pasta.

DESSERT TABLE

We invite you to indulge in the sweet finale that awaits at the dessert table. Each dessert celebrates the vibrant ingredients and culinary artistry that have made your fiesta unforgettable. In these recipes, the rich traditions of Mesoamerican, Mediterranean, and Asian flavors come together as exquisite plant-based creations, offering a perfect balance of sweetness, spice, and indulgence.

COCONUT AND AMARANTH TRES LECHES CAKE: This is a plant-based twist on the classic Tres Leches cake. It consists of a sponge cake soaked in a blend of coconut, almond, and oat milk, topped with whipped coconut cream and toasted amaranth.

CHOCOLATE AVOCADO MOUSSE WITH SPICED CHILI AND CINNAMON: This creamy mousse is made from ripe avocados, rich cacao, and a touch of agave. It is infused with a hint of chili powder and cinnamon and garnished with cacao nibs.

CHURROS WITH ORANGE BLOSSOM AND PISTACHIO SYRUP: Traditional churros are given a Mediterranean twist, drizzled with syrup made from orange blossom water and crushed pistachios, and served with a side of dark chocolate dipping sauce.

ALMOND AND DATE BAKLAVA WITH AGAVE AND CINNAMON: Layers of crispy phyllo dough are filled with a mixture of chopped almonds, dates, and a sprinkle of cinnamon. The dough is baked and then soaked in an agave-cinnamon syrup, offering a sweet and sticky treat.

MATCHA CHIA PUDDING WITH MANGO AND COCONUT: A refreshing dessert made from chia seeds soaked in almond milk and matcha powder, layered with fresh mango chunks and coconut flakes, and served chilled.

SESAME AND BLACK BEAN MOCHI WITH DARK CHOCOLATE DRIZZLE: Soft and chewy mochi made from glutinous rice flour and filled with a sweet black bean paste, finished with a drizzle of dark chocolate and a sprinkle of toasted sesame seeds.

CINNAMON-SPICED FLAN WITH FIG AND AGAVE GLAZE: This creamy plant-based flan is infused with cinnamon and topped with a fig and agave glaze, combining the flan's smooth texture with the rich sweetness of Mediterranean figs.

CHOCOLATE TAHINI TART WITH DATE AND PECAN CRUST:

A rich chocolate tart made with a creamy tahini filling, set in a date and pecan crust, topped with a sprinkle of sea salt and a drizzle of dark chocolate.

COCONUT AND LIME SORBET WITH CHILI-LIME PINEAPPLE:

This refreshing sorbet, made from coconut milk and lime juice, is served with chili-lime-spiced grilled pineapple for a sweet, tangy, and slightly spicy dessert.

SWEET POTATO AND GINGER EMPANADAS WITH CARDAMOM SUGAR:

Flaky empanadas filled with a sweet potato and ginger filling, dusted with cardamom-infused sugar, offering a warm and comforting fusion of flavors.

BEVERAGE IDEAS

No feast is complete without the perfect beverages to complement and elevate the flavors on your plate. Our carefully curated selection of drinks, inspired by the rich traditions of Mesoamerica and infused with global influences, promises to refresh, invigorate, and delight your palate. From vibrant aguas frescas to sophisticated cocktails, each beverage is crafted to enhance the dining experience and bring a touch of celebration to every sip. Let's raise our glasses and toast to the world's flavors, harmonizing for an unforgettable meal.

HIBISCUS AND TAMARIND AGUA FRESCA:

A refreshing drink made by steeping hibiscus flowers and tamarind pulp, sweetened with agave syrup, and served over ice. This slightly sweet-tart beverage is perfect for cooling down on a warm day.

CUCUMBER AND MINT LEMONADE WITH ROSE WATER:

This light and fragrant lemonade is infused with fresh cucumber slices, mint leaves, and a splash of rose water, served over ice. It combines the cooling flavors of the Mediterranean with a refreshing twist

POMEGRANATE AND ORANGE BLOSSOM ICED TEA:

Black tea brewed and chilled, mixed with pomegranate juice and a hint of orange blossom water, served with fresh pomegranate seeds and orange slices for flavor and color.

GINGER AND LEMONGRASS SPARKLING WATER:

This zesty and invigorating drink is made by infusing sparkling water with fresh ginger and lemongrass, sweetened lightly with agave syrup, and served with a twist of lime. It is both refreshing and soothing.

PRICKLY PEAR SANGRIA WITH CITRUS AND MINT:

A fusion sangria made with prickly pear juice, red wine, and a mix of Mediterranean citrus fruits (such as oranges and lemons), garnished with fresh mint leaves and served over ice for a vibrant and colorful drink.

TAMARIND AND GINGER ICED TEA:

A bold iced tea made by steeping black tea with tamarind and fresh ginger, lightly sweetened with honey or agave, and served over ice with a slice of lime for a tart and spicy kick.

MANGO LASSI WITH COCONUT AND CARDAMOM:

This creamy and tropical lassi, made with fresh mango puree, coconut yogurt, and a touch of cardamom, is blended until smooth and served chilled. It offers a delicious blend of Mesoamerican and South Asian flavors.

COCKTAIL SUGGESTIONS

COCKTAIL NAME	INGREDIENTS	INSTRUCTIONS	GARNISH
MEZCAL PINEAPPLE SMASH	- 2 oz Mezcal - 1 oz fresh pineapple juice - 0.5 oz lime juice - 0.5 oz agave syrup - Fresh cilantro and spearmint leaves	1. Muddle fresh leaves in a shaker. 2. Add mezcal, pineapple juice, lime juice, and agave syrup. 3. Fill with ice, shake well, and strain into a glass filled with ice.	Pineapple wedge dusted with chili
HIBISCUS MARGARITA	- 2 oz tequila - 1 oz hibiscus syrup (agua de jamaica) - 0.75 oz lime juice - 0.5 oz orange liqueur - Salt for rimming	1. Rim the glass with salt. 2. Combine tequila, hibiscus syrup, lime juice, and orange liqueur in a shaker. 3. Shake with ice, and strain into the salt-rimmed glass filled with ice.	Lime wheel

COCKTAIL NAME	INGREDIENTS	INSTRUCTIONS	GARNISH
TAMARIND GINGER COOLER	- 1.5 oz vodka - 1 oz tamarind concentrate - 0.5 oz ginger syrup - 0.5 oz lime juice - Club soda	1. Combine vodka, tamarind concentrate, ginger syrup, and lime juice in a shaker. 2. Shake well, strain into a glass filled with ice, and top with club soda.	Candied ginger and lime wedge
CUCUMBER MINT MOJITO	- 2 oz white rum - 1 oz lime juice - 0.75 oz agave syrup - Fresh cucumber slices - Fresh mint leaves - Club soda	1. Muddle cucumber and mint in a shaker. 2. Add rum, lime juice, and agave syrup. 3. Shake with ice, strain into a glass filled with ice, and top with club soda.	Cucumber wheel and mint sprig

COCKTAIL NAME	INGREDIENTS	INSTRUCTIONS	GARNISH
SPICED POMEGRANATE SANGRIA	- 1 bottle of red wine - 1 cup pomegranate juice - 0.5 cup brandy - 0.25 cup orange liqueur - 1 orange, sliced - 1 apple, diced - Pomegranate seeds - 2 cinnamon sticks - 1 star anise - Sparkling water (optional)	1. Combine red wine, pomegranate juice, brandy, and orange liqueur in a pitcher. 2. Add fruit, cinnamon sticks, and star anise. 3. Chill for 2 hours, serve over ice.	Orange slices and pomegranate seeds

CREATE, COLLECT & FUSE IDEAS

CRAFT YOUR CULINARY JOURNEY